THE VOICE OF THE SPIRIT

The Spirituality of St. John of the Cross

THE VOICE OF THE SPIRIT

THE SPIRITUALITY OF ST. JOHN OF THE CROSS

Edited and Introduced by

ELIZABETH HAMILTON

OUR SUNDAY VISITOR, Inc.
NOLL PLAZA, HUNTINGTON, IN 46750

First published in Great Britain in 1976 by Darton, Longman and Todd, Ltd., 85 Gloucester Road, London SW7 4SU

This edition published by arrangement with Darton, Longman and Todd, Ltd.

ISBN: 0-87973-686-0
Library of Congress Catalog Card Number: 76-53609

Cover Design by Eric Nesheim

Published, printed and bound in the U.S.A. by
Our Sunday Visitor, Inc.
Noll Plaza
Huntington, Indiana 46750

686

CONTENTS

AUTHOR'S NOTE

The translations from the Spanish are my own with the exception of the poems which have been specially translated for this book by Richard Austin.

I owe Mr Austin a particular debt of gratitude for so kindly undertaking this work.

I am grateful to Fr Anselm O.D.C. for his advice and help while I was preparing this book for publication.

So as not to distort the message in the passages from which the excerpts have been chosen, I have taken the liberty, here and there, of omitting or inserting a word or phrase where I thought this necessary.

Elizabeth Hamilton

ABBREVIATIONS

A.M.C. *The Ascent of Mount Carmel*
D.N.S. *The Dark Night of the Soul*
S.C. *The Spiritual Canticle*
L.F.L. *The Living Flame of Love*
S.S.M. *Spiritual Sentences and Maxims* collected by
   P. Andrés de la Encarnación.
P.L. *Points of Love*

PART ONE

Introduction

> En el principio moraba
> El Verbo, y en Dios vivía,
> En quien su felicidad
> Infinita poseía
>
> In the beginning lived
> The Word, and in God resided,
> And His joy in him
> From infinity abided.

These are the opening lines of a poem in which St John of the Cross meditates on the Trinity.

The thought of this sixteenth-century Carmelite mystic and poet is steeped in the Scriptures. He kept in his cell, a contemporary recalls, one book only: a Bible – this and a painted crucifix. We hear, too, of his singing psalms while he journeyed over the Sierras, and reading the Bible as he walked along the banks of the Tagus.

His teaching on prayer is founded on the Scriptures. Prayer is not to be thought of in terms of pious exercises or vain repetitions. It is a way of life, an attitude permeating our lives at every level, reaching to the very depths of our being. 'He who would come after me let

him deny himself and take up his cross and follow me.'
To where do we follow the Master? To Calvary? Certainly, but that is not the end of our journey. The Crucifixion has meaning only as a prelude to the Resurrection and the coming down of the Holy Spirit at Pentecost.

If, therefore, we want to understand what John of the Cross is saying we must not stop short when we have read *The Ascent of Mount Carmel* and *The Dark Night of the Soul.* We must read *The Spiritual Canticle* and *The Living Flame of Love,* dwell upon the joy, the ecstasy of which these speak.

This teaching St John has expressed in a manner uniquely his own – one which, if it is to be understood, must be seen against the background not only of his native Castile, but sixteenth-century Spain in general. It was, in fact, a world that bore certain resemblances to our own – one in which extremes of prosperity and destitution existed side by side. Doña Teresa de Cepeda y Ahumada, better known as St Teresa of Ávila, was brought up in a *palacio* bearing on its frontage the family escutcheon. Her father wore crimson and violet doublets stitched with gold. Juan de Yepes y Álvarez, that is St John of the Cross, was born in a dusty *pueblo* on the Castilian plain, in poverty so great that his widowed mother, because she had not the wherewithal to feed and clothe her little son, had to lodge him in an orphanage. Extremes were woven into the pattern of life : *todo o nada.* All or nothing. Heat or cold. Light or darkness. Truth or falsehood. God or the devil.

It was the age of the *conquistadores,* many of whom, having set out for the New World in a spirit of adventure, fired, in some instances, with ideals, came back corrupted by materialism, enriched by the spoils of their victims to whose fate they showed a callous indifference.

It was a world in which genuine mysticism rubbed shoulders with self-induced mystical experience – even cynicism. Reflect upon the *caballeros* in El Greco's mural in the church of Santo Tomé in Toledo. You will see gravity, piety, spirituality, but also, if you study the painting more carefully, a suggestion of pious posturing, worldly calculation and that delicate compromising with truth which Teresa deplored.*

En el principio. . . . In the beginning was the Word. And the Word was made flesh. Christ stripping himself of the glory of the Godhead became like us in all things, sin excepted. He who was the Light of the world surrendered himself to the darkness of faith, trusting to the Father, conforming his will to that of the Father. He suffered ignominy, rejection, physical and mental anguish. And yet he is the bringer of the Good News, an exemplar of hope and joy. His death on the cross is not a tragedy. It is a triumph culminating with the glory of the Resurrection and, radiating from the Resurrection, ever widening circles of light, so that in and through Christ all creation is illumined.

In *The Ascent of Mount Carmel* and *The Dark Night*

* *St Teresa and Her Reform* by Fr Anselm O.D.C. in *St Teresa of Ávila,* edited by Fr Thomas O.D.C., and Fr Gabriel O.D.C., Clonmore & Reynolds, Dublin 1963, p. 24.

of the Soul St John traces a journey made in the darkness of faith – a darkness which is not negative, but positive; not an end, but a means to an end. It is the faith that St Paul calls the substance of things hoped for, the evidence of things not seen. The demands implicit in this journey are uncompromising, in that there is asked of us the rejection, the negation, of all that is not God. Only by emptying ourselves of that which is not God can we be filled with God. And this emptying is accomplished in two ways : actively by our own efforts; passively when God himself, independent of anything we can do, works upon the soul.

This emptiness attained and the soul cleared of dross, we are free to embrace in our love not God in isolation but his entire creation. It is a matter of perspective. If God is given first place in our hearts and minds then we can recover all that we renounced – enjoy it with an intensity unknown before. Indeed, the dark night of faith takes us a step further in the liberation begun with baptism which, setting free the soul from the power of the devil, enables us, through the Holy Spirit, to become the children of God. The joy and fulness of life that is the fruit of this liberation finds expression in *The Spiritual Canticle* and *The Living Flame of Love*. Darkness has given place to day. Before, we could not bear the brilliance of this light. We were dazzled, as owls whose eyes are blinded by the brilliance of the sun.

It is not a matter of St John, as a writer, having undergone a change of mood. No, the joy of which he tells goes deeper : it emanates from the union forged between the Beloved (the soul) and the Lover (God) – whether the awareness of this union be no more than a passing, transient moment or, in what mystics call the spiritual marriage, a state of happiness without end. In this union, creation, aglow like a burning log, is illumined by the fire of the Holy Spirit. All is lit with an incandescence which is nothing other than God's immanence.

In a remarkable stanza in *The Spiritual Canticle* God is identified with the mountains, the wooded valleys, strange islands (suggested to the saint by tales perhaps brought back by the *conquistadores*), roaring rivers, the whisper of caressing breezes :

> *Mi Amado, las montañas,*
> *Los valles solitarios nemorosos,*
> *Las ínsulas extrañas*
> *Los ríos sonorosos,*
> *El silbo de los aires amorosos.*

Has this Doctor of the Church, this theologian of the highest order, lapsed into pantheism? Not at all. He is speaking here not as a theologian, but as a poet and mystic, swept aloft to heights of ecstasy beyond the power of words to scale.

*

St John is called the doctor of love. Moreover the reality of the love that can unite the soul to God becomes more intelligible, more alive, because the Saint, drawing upon (not slavishly echoing) the *Song of Songs,* presents his teaching in imagery – and with a psychological slant – that holds good for love on the human level : a readiness to sacrifice all for the beloved; a capacity to endure the seemingly unendurable. The soul on its dark journey encounters obstacles, misgivings, doubts, fears, anxieties, but these, as in human love, if the lovers are faithful, culminate in the light and the joy of fulfilment. Further, this joy, because it is established on firm foundations, is one which leaves the soul (or, if you prefer, the person) free to experience, within the compass of our love of God and God's love for us, a heightened love for his creation at every level whether human beings or the world of nature.

Sensitive to the beauty of nature, sensitive, too, to the needs of others, deeply compassionate, St John writes nevertheless with an astringency which may deter, even alarm, some readers. Yet the purpose of the saint, who is sometimes called the doctor of *nada* (nothingness), is not to impose an inhuman deprivation, but rather to show us how, the clouds that dim our vision having been dispelled, we can attain our true end : union with God. It is essential to read St John of the Cross in his wholeness. Words wrested out of context can give an imbalance, indeed a totally distorted picture. William James and J. K. Huysmans looked upon St John as a fanatic, indeed a kind of fakir – Huysmans described him as one who at the end of his journey is 'terrible and bleeding, with unbowed head'. Dean Inge deplored the Saint's 'cruelty to his soul'. Bishop John Robinson in

Exploration Into God, commenting on a passage, applies the word 'terrifying' – and terrifying the passage is, if read in isolation. To others, however, the Saint's writing affords a welcome corrective to the sometimes sugary style of Thérèse of Lisieux or the ebullience of Teresa of Ávila.

Regrettably some of St John's warmest admirers have done him little service. One need only think of statues representing an emaciated, forbidding figure embracing a cross of exaggerated proportions. Then, again, books about St John – even some of the better ones – tend to impose a stereotyped, hagiographical pattern, giving a picture of a 'ready-made' saint, devoid of human frailties and shortcomings. As a little boy John fell into a pond, then seeing a lady on the bank reaching out her arms to help him, hesitated to put his grubby hands into hers. Predictably the hagiographers conclude the lady to have been the Blessed Virgin. Possibly the boy believed this to be so. Nevertheless a contemporary, who had the story from the lips of the Saint, says that he came ashore by supporting himself on a plank. To another contemporary, St John related the incident without mention of Our Lady.

When he was a novice John was so openly and tactlessly critical of what he regarded as the laxity of his brethren that his censorious attitude made him thoroughly disliked. At the sight of him they used to scatter saying: 'Here comes the devil'. Some biographers, instead of seeing this 'holier than thou' attitude for what it is worth – the smug, over-zealous piety of a very young religious, present it as a pointer to sanctity.

*

St John of the Cross can justifiably be called the doctor of spiritual maturity. Our faith, he stresses, is founded on Christ. Through Christ his Son, God the Father has spoken to us once and for all. We need no props, supports, or spiritual 'consolations'. As to visions, locutions and the like, which in sixteenth-century Spain appear to have been the order of the day, such phenomena, he says (even at the risk of their having come from God) are best ignored. Superfluities discarded, the soul must cease to experience God in the manner of a helpless child. In his emphasis on the need to discard infantile attitudes he teaches that, just as the time comes for a mother to put down her child out of her arms and allow him to walk on his own feet, so God wills that the soul shall learn to go forward to maturity. Indeed, in this, St John's teaching recalls ideas found in the writings of Dietrich Bonhoeffer who argues that an immature attitude conditions man to think of God in terms of a *deus ex machina* ready to solve all mysteries, provide all answers. The author of *The Dark Night of the Soul* could have written Bonhoeffer's words: 'The God who is with us is the God who has forsaken us'. We must live at times, both writers imply, as though (to quote St Augustine) God were not here – and yet he is here, always at hand.

What St John of the Cross calls 'spiritual gluttony'

18

was repellent to him: the attitude of those whose 'devotion' is centred not on God but on irrelevances – elaborately fashioned rosaries, over-decorated oratories; a concern not that Mass be celebrated, but at what precise hour, by what particular priest, with how many candles and such like.

When attending a Chapter at Lisbon he resolutely refused to accompany some of his brethren to visit a nun renowned for her bleeding wounds. 'We should put our trust in the wounds of Christ alone,' he said. Instead of visiting the nun he walked on the banks of the Tagus reading his Bible. He said that the nun was an impostor. This proved to be so.

*

St John of the Cross is in his own genre a poet of the highest order. But he is not an easy poet. How could he be, impelled as he was to attempt the impossible – to express in words the ineffable; to convey in language an awareness of God's presence uniquely his own, going beyond anything experienced by the majority of his readers and at times baffling even to himself? Questioned about his poems he confessed that there were moments when he himself scarcely knew what he was saying. Moreover, whereas at one time he had to search for words, at another they came unbidden. Any creative artist will understand this. The muse comes and goes, now inspiring the artist, now abandoning him to his own devices. And St John's muse was the Holy Spirit.

Poems such as his cannot be analysed on a purely

intellectual level. They have to be absorbed, pondered, listened to as one listens to a melody of Mozart or the throbbing, ecstatic song of a lark soaring heavenward. They have a strange dreamlike quality, reminiscent now of certain passages in the Hebrew prophets or the Apocalypse, now of such poets as Christopher Smart, William Blake, Gerard Manley Hopkins and T. S. Eliot – what Fr Martin D'Arcy calls an 'unearthly glow', a 'strange quality which invades the images and persuades [the reader] that there must be a love which is a secret between God and the soul'.* When for a while St John was confessor to the Carmelite nuns at the convent of the Incarnation at Ávila, the sisters, charmed by the music of the words, used to learn stanzas by heart. Moreover it was largely as a result of questions put to him by these and other sisters that he wrote his commentaries on the poems – works which were intended to throw light on the poems, not become a substitute for them. Somewhat cumbersome at times, uneven in the quality of the writing, marred, it might be argued, by lengthy digressions (he examines, for example, the harm done by inadequate and clumsy spiritual directors) the commentaries are invaluable for their theological and their psychological content, for flashes of humour, for colourful, often down to earth, imagery, and, perhaps most of all, for the light they throw on Spain at that era.

*

* *Poems of St John of the Cross* with translation by Roy Campbell, Harvill Press, preface, p. 7.

St John of the Cross, Juan de Yepes y Álvarez, was born in 1542 at Fontiveros, a straggling *pueblo* built of sun-baked clay, between Ávila and Salamanca. In winter it is exposed to the full blast of shrilling winds, in summer to parching sun. Away in the distance the Sierras de Gredos rise sharp against the sky.

John's father, Gonzalo de Yepes, a young man of breeding with a prosperous future ahead of him, came into disfavour with his relations when he fell in love with and married Catalina Álvarez, an orphan whom he met at Fontiveros when lodging at a *telar* or workshop where she earned her living as a weaver. Cut off by his family, Gonzalo made his home at Fontiveros and, like his wife, became a weaver. Some twelve years later, shortly after the birth of John he died, leaving a widow and three sons in a state of extreme poverty. Luis, the second son, died. Then, in 1551 Catalina moved to Medina del Campo where she continued to earn a meagre living, sharing her home with her eldest son Francisco, and his wife. So straitened were her circumstances that she had to lodge her youngest child, John, in a nearby orphanage where he was fed, clothed and taught to read and write.

John having proved unsatisfactory as an apprentice to a carpenter, a wood-carver then a printer, finally found employment in a hospital, where he slept and worked in the wards, as well as collecting alms in the streets. Antonio Álvarez de Toledo, the superintendent of the hospital, noticing the boy's unusual intelligence, enrolled him at a near-by *colegio* founded by the Jesuits.

John's work at the hospital meant that he had to miss many classes. But he made up for this by assiduous study. He used to work far into the night by the dim light of a *candela* or small oil lamp.

In due course Álvarez de Toledo suggested that, should John decide to become a priest, he could be given a chaplaincy at the hospital. It was a tempting offer, but the young man had his mind on other things. One night (he was now twenty-one) he knocked on the door of the Carmelite College of Santa Ana in Medina del Campo, where a year later he made his profession. The following year, November 1564, on the strength of his exceptional proficiency in the Latin language he was admitted to the University of Salamanca, then at the height of its fame.

When he returned to Medina del Campo in the early autumn of 1567, he intended to become a Carthusian. This, however, was not to be. For at Medina he became acquainted with Teresa of Ávila who had recently founded there the second convent of her Reform. Anxious to extend this Reform to friars as well as nuns, she asked John why he should want to become a Carthusian when his own Order was crying out for men of courage and enterprise. Would he not, she suggested, become one of the first friars of the Reform? She had already won over Antonio de Heredia, a man in his sixties, but wanted to bring in young men. John fell in with her wishes, having stipulated with characteristic firmness that he would do as she wished only provided that he was not kept waiting long.

The meeting with Teresa was a turning point in his life. She was enchanted with her 'little Seneca', a friar 'small in stature but great in the eyes of God'. Each proved a match for the other in strength of character. When John was with Teresa at the time of making her third foundation at Valladolid she wrote of disagreements between the two 'on business and other matters', but went on to say that the fault was hers. Another time when as a kind of literary diversion she asked for expositions on the words : 'Seek yourself in me', she said tartly, when commenting on John's contribution, 'God deliver us from those who would turn everything into the highest level of contemplation'. And another time : 'It's useless to try to talk to Fray John of the Cross – he goes into a trance and takes you with him'. These 'differences' were on the surface. Basically each esteemed the other. John treasured for years the many letters he had received from Teresa. He destroyed them only because he feared they would fall into the wrong hands.

In November 1568 John was clothed in the rough frieze habit made for him by St Teresa herself. Soon afterwards along with Fray Antonio he was installed in the first house for friars of the Reform : a tumbledown farm building at Duruelo, a few miles from Fontiveros. In Advent of that year Mass was said in what Teresa calls 'That little Bethlehem'. Conditions were indeed primitive. As a choir a loft was used, padded with straw against the cold. Even so snowflakes drifted in, settling on the friars' habits. Moreover the roof was so low that it was necessary to sit or lie – it was impossible to stand. The many crosses and skulls in the chapel were a mark, in Teresa's eyes, of true devotion. At the sight of them, she writes, two friends of hers, merchants who had travelled with her from Medina, were so affected that 'they could no nothing but weep'. But what impressed her most was a drawing depicting Christ on the Cross, pinned above the holy water stoop – it was more moving, she wrote, than any crucifix of the finest workmanship. There is every reason to suppose that this was the work of St John of the Cross. He was an artist as well as a poet. At the convent of the Incarnation, Ávila, you are shown a pen-and-ink sketch which inspired Salvador Dali's painting, 'El Cristo'. The figure hanging on the cross is viewed from the side (below the level of the observer), the head sunk on to the chest, the hair falling forward, the knees bent beneath the weight of the body. St John also made drawings illustrating the stages of the Ascent of Mount Carmel. He gave them to nuns to keep in their missals.

The period during which John, at the suggestion of St Teresa, was confessor at the Incarnation was valuable to him. He had time for reflection, but it also enabled him to have more to do with women than previously. He treated the nuns with firmness, good sense, gentleness, and understanding. His handling of a girl living in the neighbourhood who, infatuated by him, forced her way in when he was having supper alone, shows his imperturbability. Unlike St Kevin, who from his rocky retreat at Glendalough, hurled an intruding female into the lake below, St John spoke to the girl with quiet reasonableness and sent her away, her mind at peace. He used to talk freely of this incident.

All was going well at the Incarnation when there came a bolt from the blue. As a consequence of one of the unedifying disputes (St Teresa speaks of 'a great storm of trials') prevalent at that time between the Calced Carmelites and the Discalced, or Carmelites of Teresa's Reform, John was kidnapped by the former.*

After first being confined in Medina del Campo he was imprisoned in the monastery of the Calced at Toledo. His cell, a cramped, cupboard-like room, six feet by ten, was lit by a narrow opening so high in the wall that, to read his office, he had to stand on a bench and hold up his book to the light. He slept on the floor, on a board, his covering two shabby blankets. Damp seeped from the stone. In winter he was chilled to the marrow, in summer, stifled. Only during the latter part of his imprisonment, when a young compassionate gaoler was put in charge, was he allowed a change of tunic. His food was scraps of bread and an occasional sardine. On fast days he was taken to the refectory where he ate on the floor, like a dog. As he did so the Prior upbraided him for his iniquities, specially his pride and obstinacy, after which his brethren walked around him lashing his bare shoulders with a cane and reciting the *Miserere*.

* See *St Teresa and Her Reform* by Fr Anselm O.D.C., in *St Teresa of Ávila* edited by Fr Thomas O.D.C., and Fr Gabriel O.D.C., Clonmore & Reynolds 1963, pp. 17–20.

John, though he had acted in good faith, was juridically at fault in that he had ignored orders to return to a convent of the Calced. Moreover his treatment during his imprisonment was probably no worse than that meted out at the time to secular offenders. This, however, only raises the embarrassing question as to why 'devout' Christians, despite the teaching of the gospel, so often prove incapable of rising above the *mores* of the society in which they find themselves.

As well as physical maltreatment John had to listen to Carmelites in an adjoining room saying, for his benefit, that this prisoner would leave his place of confinement only to be buried; that he and Teresa of Ávila were heretics; that possibly the best thing would be to drown him in a well.

And all the time he heard far below the sinister roar of the river Tagus coursing between steep, echoing rocks – a roar that in winter became a veritable crescendo.

John's escape from prison makes a dramatic story. Details sometimes conflict but in the main the facts are clear.

The young gaoler (the one who had provided a change of tunic) moved with compassion, made a practice, while the community were having their siesta, of leaving open the door of the cell so that his prisoner might get a breath of air. Taking advantage of this, John used to venture tentatively outside and gradually familiarised himself with the layout of the monastery, weighing, as he did so, the possibilities of escape. Also he worked at the nails fastening the padlock of the door until they became so loose that the padlock, if given a push, could be dislodged.

En una noche oscura. At dead of night on 16 August 1578, having made himself a rope from strips torn from his blankets, he opened the door. The padlock fell to the floor with a crash, wakening visitors in an adjoining room. All, he thought, was ruined. However the visitors, after some grumbling and snorting, were soon asleep again. John clambered out of a window on to a small balcony, flung his habit down below and, having made fast his rope to a rail proceeded to slide down, gripping the rope between his hands and knees. The rope however was not long enough : he had to jump the last six feet or so. He landed on the top of a wall strewn with stones – just where his habit had fallen. A full moon shone. Immediately below, the Tagus roared. If he had jumped a yard or two further forward, he would have been dashed on the rocks forming the gorge.

He put on his habit, scrambled along the wall, presently dropped into a courtyard from which, to his dismay, he could find no exit : a wall, which in his weak condition, he could not surmount, closed him in on four sides. His anguish was overwhelming. What precisely happened at this point is not clear. But whether by sheer perseverance and ingenuity or, as some say, through the intervention of the Blessed Virgin, he eventually landed in the street and in the early hours of the morning presented himself at the convent of the Discalced Carmelites. There the nuns kept him in hiding until Don Pedro González de Mendoza, a canon of Toledo Cathedral and a friend of the nuns, took him to the Hospital de la Santa Cruz of which he was administrator. John was scarcely more than a hundred yards from the place of his imprisonment, but he was free.

Witnesses at the processes for the canonisation of St John spoke of the graces and spiritual consolations he received while in prison. Others told of his intense suffering in mind and body, his aridity and his desolation of soul. One would expect, in a man of his sensitivity, reactions to vary from day to day, hour to hour. One thing we know – during this period when every indignity was heaped upon him he wrote the greater part of the joyous, even ecstatic *Spiritual Canticle*, the beginning, probably, of *The Ascent of Mount Carmel*, and a number of shorter poems.

Undoubtedly imprisonment was for him a traumatic experience. It left its mark on his personality not only in the form of a greater maturity and tolerance, but also on the creative level. He proved himself one of those artists who, far from being the slave of circumstances, derive inspiration directly or often indirectly from personal anguish : experiences which would have caused some to be deranged, found an outlet – indeed a catharsis – in creativity.

*

From the time he had received his habit from the hands of Teresa of Ávila, St John devoted himself unsparingly to the service of the Discalced Carmelites. In October 1578, after being released from prison he was appointed vicar to the priory of Monte Calvario. Much as he was inspired by the beauty of the Andalusian landscape, he was, like Teresa, truly Castilian in his attitude to Andalusia – he was not wholly at his ease in this region of Spain where he was destined to pass long stretches of time. In 1579 he founded a Discalced house in Baeza, of which he was rector. In June 1582 he helped Ana de Jesús, one of Teresa's most esteemed nuns, in founding a convent at Granada, and was elected prior of Los Mártires. He attended many chapters, including those of Almodóvar, Lisbon and Valladolid, and in 1588 was appointed first Definitor to the Order. Left to his own devices, this poet and mystic liked to roam the Sierras, sit by a stream watching fish darting in the water, look out at night from the window of his cell at flowers pale beneath the starlit darkness. Inevitably, however, he was caught in a whirl of activity, and if this was not of his choosing he welcomed it as a means of serving his brethren : in the contemplative life, prayer, he believed, and the service of our neighbour are two sides to the same coin. Less welcome was the jealousy, ill-will, and calumny to which he was consistently exposed, because he had the courage to speak the truth regardless of whether it was acceptable or not.

There is ample evidence as to St John's qualities as a superior. He was no longer the censorious youth who had infuriated his companions. He treated his friars with gentleness and respect. Nothing, he used to say, more effectively shows a man's unworthiness to hold office than an imperious manner; if someone must be reprimanded, 'we should do our best', he said, 'to see that such a person does not go away dispirited'.

He attached great importance to courtesy among religious. If courtesy, he said, were lost to the Order that would be a major disaster. Courtesy, he believed, was an essential facet in the Christian life and, therefore, in religion.

He himself, however, was not always treated with the courtesy by which he set such store. Having arrived at a religious house one evening, exhausted from his journey (it was a season of grilling heat), he was greeted enthusiastically by the community who thronged around him, asking for his blessing. The Prior, however – a boorish man – interfered. They had no business, he said, to be talking after Compline – he would not permit it, whoever the visitor might be. John without any show of displeasure at once fell silent and withdrew although, as a Definitor, he was the Prior's superior and, what is more, not long before this, the same prior had been among his novices.

He was deeply concerned for persons as individuals. If one of his community was depressed he would persuade him to come out with him and walk over the Sierras. If one was ill he would himself cook the invalid some tasty dish and sit by his bed, coaxing him to eat. His sympathy for the sick owed something perhaps to the years in boyhood when he worked in a hospital. Also, though he had extraordinary stamina, extraordinary resilience, he knew what it meant to be unwell. A somewhat endearing story tells how, when feeling ill during a journey, he confessed that the one thing he fancied was some asparagus. 'But it isn't the season for asparagus,' his companion reminded him. 'Besides, it doesn't grow in these parts.' Shortly afterwards the two men were taking a siesta on a river bank when they noticed a bunch of asparagus lying on a stone in the water. John asked his comrade to fetch it and to leave on the stone a *quadro* in payment, in case the owner should return. The narrator of this story vouches for its veracity: 'I *know* it's true, for it was *I* who prepared the asparagus!'

*

St John's outspokenness, coupled with a determination to maintain in the Order the moderation and good sense advocated by St Teresa brought him into increasing ill-favour. In June 1591 at the chapter-general held in Madrid he was stripped of all offices and sent as an ordinary friar to Peñuela, near Baeza.

He arrived on 10 August, but shortly afterwards fell ill. A high fever accompanied by inflammation indicated an infection of the blood. He went on, therefore, another five miles to Ubeda, where there were doctors.

This was on 22 September. His health, however, did not improve. Indeed his physical sufferings were intensified by the callous treatment meted out by a churlish prior. Even so he maintained a tranquillity which finally put to shame even the prior. On 14 December he repeatedly asked what was the time. 'Tonight,' he said, 'I shall say matins in heaven'. His condition deteriorating, his brethren gathered around his bed and recited the

De Profundis and the *Miserere*. Afterwards he asked them to read some verses from the *Song of Songs*. 'What pearls beyond price', he murmured. The clock struck midnight. He folded his hands and closed his eyes. It was the hour for matins.

He was buried in the chapel.

One night, the story goes, when, after the lamps had been extinguished, the monks were making a meditation, they were suddenly aware of a radiance illumining the darkness. It came from the tomb of St John.

PART TWO

Excerpts from the writings of St John of the Cross

I

THE ASCENT OF MOUNT CARMEL AND THE DARK NIGHT OF THE SOUL

Song of the soul having attained union with God
by the way of spiritual negation

Within the shadowed night,
My cares enflamed in fire,
(O joyous flight!)
When no one was in sight,
I crept away when all the house was still.

Secure in my disguise,
Up the secret stairs I climbed,
(O blissful enterprise!)
Hidden from all watchful eyes,
While those within in silence slept.

In that blessed night,
So secret and unseen,
I went with no other light
Than of my heart, whose gleam
Led me alone in its sight.

It blazed and showed the way,
Brighter than the dazzle of high noon,
To where the loved one lay
Whom I had so surely known,
Where there was no one else to be found.

O night that led my eyes,
O darkness, better loved than morning skies,
O night that clasped the lover
To his bride, each of them transfigured
Into ecstasies such as love all lovers unifies.

Within the flowering of my soul
Which for himself he tended whole,
He closed at last his sleeping eyes,
And I gave to him all that I owned
As gently as in the air the cedar sighs.

Around the battlements sped
The wind to spread his fine hair wide,
With his gentle hand
My throat he pierced, and
All my senses then were atrophied.

Lost to myself alone,
My face pressed upon his own,
I ceased all that I endeavoured,
And from me all cares I severed,
To toss them to the lilies there to die.

THE DARK NIGHT

The Voice of the Holy Spirit . . .

To expound and describe the dark night through which
the soul must pass if it is to attain the divine light of
perfect union with God in love (as far, that is, as is
possible on earth) I would need a knowledge and
experience beyond anything that is mine. For the darkness and trials, spiritual and temporal, through which
privileged beings usually have to pass if they are to
reach this exalted degree of perfection, are so many and
so profound that human knowledge does not suffice for
us to put these into words. Only he who himself passes
this way can understand and not even he has the
language in which to tell of such things.

This being so, in saying a little about the dark night
I shall not depend either on experience or knowledge,
since both may falter and deceive. While not omitting to
resort to these in so far as I can, in all that (with God's
help) I have to say, or at least in what is most important
and dark to the understanding, I shall avail myself of
Holy Scripture. If we take the Scriptures for our guide,
we shall not go astray, since he who speaks to us through
them is none other than the Holy Spirit.

A. M. C. Prologue

The dark night . . .

To attain a state of perfection a soul normally has to
pass through two principal kinds of night which those

versed in the spiritual life call purgations or purifications. Here, we use the word 'night', for in each the soul journeys as if by night, in darkness.

The first night, or purgation, affects the sensual part of the soul; the second, the spiritual.

The first, which pertains to beginners, occurs at the time when God proceeds to bring them into the state of contemplation. The second, which pertains to those who are already somewhat advanced, occurs when God wants to lead them to union with himself.

A.M.C. II i-iii

There are three reasons, we may say, for using the word 'night' to describe the journey made by the soul to union with God.

The first concerns the point of departure. For the soul, as it goes forth, must, by denying itself all worldly things, totally renounce the desire for these : this denial and deprivation are, so to speak, night to man's senses. The second concerns the manner, or road, by which the soul must travel to this union – that is, faith, which also is as dark as night to the understanding.

The third concerns the point towards which the soul journeys – that is, God, who equally, in this life, is darkness to the soul. These three nights have to pass through the soul, or rather the soul must pass through these, if it is to come to union with God.

A.M.C. I II i

In the book of the holy Tobias these nights were fore-shadowed by the three which were to pass (so the angel commanded) before the young Tobias should be unified to his bride.

A.M.C. I II ii

Tenebrae eam non comprehenderunt

The affection the soul feels for created things is pitch darkness in the eyes of God, and when the soul is clothed in this affection it is totally unable – unless it first cast these from it – to be enlightened and possessed by the pure, unclouded light of God. For light cannot be in harmony with darkness. As St John the Evangelist says : *'Tenebrae eam non comprehenderunt.* The darkness could not grasp the light.'

Two contraries, philosophy teaches, cannot coexist in one person. The darkness which is attachment to creatures and the light which is God are contrary to each other, and have no resemblance, nor do they accord one with the other, as St Paul made clear to the Corinthians : *'Quae conventio luci ad tenebras?* What have light and darkness in common?' Hence the light of divine union cannot dwell in the soul unless these attach-ments have first taken flight.

A.M.C. I IV i-ii

Darkness was under his feet . . .

St Paul says: 'Whosoever would be united to God must
believe.' That is, he must walk by faith and faith alone,
his understanding shrouded in darkness. For, below this
darkness, the understanding is united with God. Beneath
it God is hidden, even as David says: 'Darkness was
under his feet. And he rose upon the cherubim and flew
upon the wings of the wind. And he made darkness his
hiding place and the water dark.'

A.M.C. II IX i

Faith: light and darkness . . .

Faith, the theologians say, is a habit of the soul that is
both certain and obscure. It is obscure in that it enables
us to believe truths revealed by God himself which
transcend all natural light, surpass all human understanding. Hence, this overwhelming light of faith which
is bestowed upon the soul is thick darkness, for it overwhelms that which is great, blots out that which is small,
even as the light of the sun overwhelms all other lights,
so that when it shines and destroys our power of vision
these others no longer appear to be lights at all.

A.M.C. II III i

The devil . . .

In this dark night it is usual for the devil to fill persons with presumption and pride. Influenced by vanity and arrogance they allow themselves to be involved in external behaviour which gives an impression of holiness – raptures, for instance, and other such phenomena.

D.N.S. II II iii

Some reach such a pitch of evil that they want no one to appear good except themselves. Consequently, whenever the opportunity arises they condemn and slander others, seeing the mote in the eye of another, while blind to the beam in their own : they strain at another's gnat but themselves swallow a camel.

D.N.S. I II ii

PSYCHIC PHENOMENA

Imaginary Visions

These can be actively produced in the soul through its own operation beneath forms, figures and images . . . We imagine Christ crucified or bound to the column. We imagine God enthroned in majesty. Or we visualise glory as a splendid radiance or something of the kind. Or we picture all sorts of other things, divine or human, which come within the scope of the imagination. Now, all these pictures must be cast out from the soul.

. . . This is because the imagination cannot fashion or picture anything other than that which it has experienced through the exterior senses – that is, what it has seen with the eyes, heard with the ears, and so on. At most it can only evoke likenesses of things it has seen, heard or felt, which are of no more consequence than those which have been received by the senses nor even of as much consequence. For although, having seen gold and pearls, we can imagine palaces made of pearls and whole mountains of gold, all this is less than the essence of a little gold or one pearl, despite the fact that in the imagination the quantity and beauty are far greater. And since no created things, as I have said, can bear any proportion to the being of God, it follows that nothing we imagine in their likeness can serve as a proximate means to union with God. Quite the contrary.

Those, therefore, who visualise God under any of these likenesses or as a great fire or a radiance or any other such form and who think that anything of this kind resembles him, are indeed far from drawing near to him. For although these likenesses, appearances and forms of meditation, are needful for beginners – that they may little by little, through the senses, feed and fire the soul with love – and although these may serve as a remote means of union with God, through which persons have often to pass in order to reach their goal and attain repose of spirit, yet such persons must do no more than pass through these, not remain in them. Otherwise they will not reach their goal, which has no resemblance to these remote means nor anything to do with them.

The steps leading up a staircase have nothing in common with the landing at the top or the room to which this landing leads, yet they are a means of reaching both. If the person going up did not leave the stairs behind until there were no more steps to climb, but chose to remain on any one of them, he would not reach the landing nor the restful room to which he looks forward. Likewise the soul that is to attain in life the union of supreme repose and blessing by means of these steps of meditation, forms and ideas, must pass through these and have done with them, for they bear no resemblance to, no proportion to, the goal which is God. Hence St Paul in the Acts of the Apostles: *'Non debemus aestimare auro vel argento aut lapidi sculpturae artis, et cogitationis hominis, divinum esse similem*: We ought not to think of the Godhead by likening him to gold or silver neither to stone that is shaped in the hand of an artist nor to anything man can conceive in his imagination.'

Great, therefore, is the error of certain spiritual persons who have tried to draw near to God by means of images, forms and meditations suited to beginners. It is God's intention to lead them on to greater spiritual blessings, which are within and invisible, by taking from them the pleasure and the attraction of discursive meditations. Such persons, however, either cannot or dare not cut themselves off from palpable methods to which they have become accustomed.

A.M.C. II XII iii-vi

Peter had no doubt whatsoever as to the vision of the glorified Christ which he saw at the Transfiguration, yet when he described it in his second canonical Epistle, he did not want this to be regarded as an important and certain testimony. It was to faith that he directed his hearers : *Et habemus firmiorem propheticum sermonem: cui benefacitis attendentes, quasi lucernae lucenti in caliginoso loco, donec dies elucescat.* We have, he means, a more sure testimony than this vision on Mount Tabor – the sayings and words of the prophets who bear testimony to Christ. It is to these we must pay unswerving attention, as to a lamp which gives light in a dark room.

If we ponder on this comparison we shall find there the message we are giving. For in telling us to look to the faith of which the prophets spoke, as to a lamp shining in a dark room, Peter is bidding us stay in the darkness, our eyes closed to all other lights – telling us that in this darkness faith alone, which likewise is dark, will be the light on which we must concentrate our attention : for if we desire to concentrate on those other bright lights – the distinct lights of the understanding – we no longer give our full attention to that dark light which is faith, nor have we any longer that light in the dark room of which St Peter speaks. This room, which signifies here the understanding that is the lampstand on which the lamp is placed – must be dark until the day when the unclouded vision of God dawns upon it in the life hereafter, or, in this life, until the day of transformation and union with God towards which the soul is journeying.

A.M.C. II XVI xv

How to foil the devil

We should close our eyes to these psychic phenomena and reject them, whatever be their source. Otherwise, we are preparing the way for those that come from the devil and giving Satan such influence that not only will his visions take the place of God's, but, while his increase, those of God will decrease. And so the devil will have it all his own way. This indeed has happened to careless, ignorant persons who put such reliance on these phenomena that many have found it hard to return to God in unclouded faith.

A.M.C. II XI viii

Visions can foster complacency...

The more exterior are these corporeal forms and objects, the less profit are they to our interior and spiritual nature, because great is the distance and small the proportion existing between the corporeal and the spiritual. For although they bestow a certain amount of spirituality, as is always so when things come from God, this is much less than would be the case if these same phenomena were interior and spiritual. And so they easily become a means whereby error, presumption and pride develop; since, as they are obvious and material, they greatly stir the senses and the conclusion is drawn that they are the more important because they are the more readily experienced. Thus the soul seeks them out, believing that the light emanating from them is the guide and the means to the soul's desired goal : union with God. Yet the greater attention the soul pays to phenomena of this kind, the further it strays from the true path, the true means : faith.

Furthermore, when the soul sees such extraordinary phenomena it is often overtaken, insidiously and secretly, by a form of complacency, making it suppose it is of special importance in the sight of God – and this is contrary to humility. Also the devil knows how to insinuate into the soul a hidden self-satisfaction which at times is plain to see; he therefore often represents these things to the senses, putting before the eyes the forms of saints and wonderful lights; and, for the ears to hear, words that are cleverly dissembled; and he represents delicate perfumes, choice tastes and objects delightful to the touch, so that by nurturing a desire for such things he may lead the soul into much evil. These representations and feelings should, therefore, always be rejected. Even if some are from God, he is not displeased if they are rejected, nor is the effect, the fruit which he desires to bring about in the soul by means of these, any the less received because the soul rejects them and shows no desire for them.

A.M.C. II XI iv-v

Intellectual visions

Intellectual visions are more clear and more subtle than
those which pertain to the body. For when God grants
such a vision he bestows upon the soul a supernatural
light whereby it sees the things God wills it to see, easily
and clearly, whether they be of heaven or of earth; nor is
the absence or presence of these things a hindrance to the
vision. Sometimes it is as though a door were flung wide
open and the soul is aware of an illumination after the
manner of a flash of lightning which on a dark night
suddenly reveals objects, so that they can be seen dis-
tinctly, then plunges them in darkness, though their
shapes and appearances may remain in the memory.

A.M.C. II XXIV v

Visions falsely interpreted . . .

Words and visions coming from God may be true and
reliable and yet we ourselves be deluded through our
inability to interpret these in the sublime and important
sense which is the purpose and the meaning intended by
God. And so the safest and surest course is to encourage
people to be prudent and to flee from supernatural
phenomena – this will accustom them to a purity of
spirit in that darkness of faith which is our means of
being united to God.

A.M.C. II XIX xiv

Why it is undesirable to receive visions, even supposing they come from God

1. Faith gradually diminishes; for what is experienced through the senses detracts from faith, since faith transcends every sense. And so the soul, when it does not close its eyes to things of the senses, withdraws from means of union with God.

2. Things of the senses, if they are not rejected, are an obstacle to the spirit; for the soul rests upon them and does not soar to the invisible. This is one reason why the Lord told his disciples that he must needs go away, so that the Holy Spirit might come. Hence, too, that Magdalene might be firmly established in faith, he forbade her after his Resurrection, to touch his feet.

3. The soul becomes dependent upon these phenomena and does not advance to true contentment and detachment.

4 The soul begins to lose the favours granted by God, because it feeds upon these as though by right. But God, in giving them, does not intend that the soul should seek after them or rest in them. Indeed, it should not be presumed that such phenomena come from God.

A.M.C. II XI vii

I am aghast at what is going on these days. A person with almost no knowledge of meditation, aware during recollection of something in the nature of a locution, at once 'christens' it as coming from God. 'God said this to me . . .' 'God answered me . . .' It is quite untrue. Usually such persons are talking to themselves!

A.M.C. II XXIX iv

SPIRITUAL MATURITY

A desert land . . .

David writes of the power of the night in bringing the soul to a sublime knowledge of God: 'In the desert land, Lord, parched, dry and pathless, I appeared before you that I might behold your power and your glory.' It is wonderful indeed that David should say that the way to prepare for his knowledge of God's glory was not spiritual delights and the many pleasures he had enjoyed, but aridity and detachment from the senses, here symbolised by the dry, desert land. It is wonderful, too, that he should describe, as the road to his perception of God's power, not divine meditations and conceptions of which he had frequently made use, but his total inability to form any conception of God. . .

D.N.S. I XII vi

There is joy in heaven when God, unwrapping the soul from its swaddling clothes, puts it down out of his arms and leaves it to walk on its own feet.

D.N.S. I XII i

When I was a child . . .

'*Cum essem parvulus, loquebar ut parvulus, sapiebam ut parvulus, cogitabam ut parvulus. Quando autem factus sum vir, evacuavi quae erant parvuli.*' So says St Paul: 'When I was a child, I spoke as a child, I knew as a child, I thought as a child. But when I became a man I put away childish things.' I have explained how the things of sense and the knowledge that can be derived from them are the concern of a child. If, therefore, the soul persists in clinging to these and does not cast them aside, it will never cease to be a child: it will speak of God as a child speaks; know him as a child knows; think of him as a child thinks. For clinging to the outer husk of sense, which is the child, it will not attain the substance of the spirit which is the mature man. Thus the soul must not want these revelations to further its growth, even though God may offer them – even as a child must cease to be fed at the breast and accustom its palate to stronger, more substantial food.

A.M.C. II XVII vi

Fix your eyes on Christ alone

Under the Old Dispensation it was regarded as lawful that questions be put to God and that prophets and priests seek visions and revelations. This is because, until that time, faith had no solid foundation, neither was the law of the gospel established. It was therefore necessary for man to enquire of God and for God to speak whether by means of words, visions, revelations, figures, similitudes or the many other ways he has of giving expression to his will. For his answers, words and revelations concerned the mysteries of our faith and things touching upon this or leading to it. And since things of faith are not of man, but come from the lips of God himself, God reproached those who did not enquire from him, so that he might give them an answer and guide their concerns and happenings in the direction of faith of which they had then no knowledge because it was not yet founded.

But now when faith is established in Christ and the law of the gospel revealed, there is no need in this era of grace to enquire of God in such a manner, nor for God to speak or reply as formerly. For in giving to us, as he did, his Son who is his Word (he has no other) he spoke to each of us, once and for all, in this Word alone nor has he need to speak further.

This is the meaning of the passage with which St Paul begins when trying to persuade the Hebrews to give up their former manner of converse with God, as laid down in the law of Moses, and set their eyes on Christ alone: '*Multifariam multisque modis olim Deus loquens olim patribus in Prophetis: novissime autem diebus istis locutus est nobis in Filio*: That which God spoke of old in the prophets to our fathers in sundry ways and diverse manners, he has now at last in these days spoken once and for all in his Son.' Herein the Apostle says that God has been, as it were, dumb and has no more to say, since what he said formerly, in part, to the prophets he has now spoken to us in its entirety, in Christ – giving to us the All which is his Son.

Therefore he who would now ask anything of God or seek a vision or revelation would not only be acting foolishly, he would be offending God through not fixing his eyes wholly on Christ and seeking no new thing nor anything further. And God might answer: 'If I have spoken all things to you in my Word, which is my Son, and I have no other word, what answer can I give to you or what greater than this can I reveal to you? Fix your eyes on him alone, for in him I have spoken and revealed all things and in him you will find even more than you ask and desire. You ask for locutions and revelations, which are part, but, if you fix your eyes on him you will have the whole, for he is my complete locution and answer. He is my entire vision, my entire revelation. And so I have spoken to you, answered you, declared to you and revealed to you, in giving him as your brother, companion and master, as ransom, as reward. Since the day on which I came down upon him in my Spirit on Mount Tabor saying: *"Hic est filius meus dilectus in quo mihi bene complacui. Ipsum audite*: This is my beloved Son in whom I am well pleased: hear him,"* I have ceased from all teaching and answering and have entrusted this to him. For I have no more faith to reveal nor anything more to say . . . Ponder on this well. For you will find that in my Son all has been accomplished for you, all has been given to you – and more besides.'

A.M.C. II XXII iii-v

Consummatum est ...

The entire faith has been given to us in Christ nor is there anything further to be revealed nor ever will be. He who now craves for some supernatural enlightenment is, by implication, finding fault with God for not having given a full revelation in his Son. Although such a person may accept the faith and believe it, he is nevertheless showing a curiosity which betrays a lack of faith. We must not expect to be granted instruction or anything else in a supernatural manner. For when Christ died on the Cross, saying '*Consummatum est*, It is finished', an end was made of all the forms and rites and ceremonial of the Old Law. We must now, therefore, be guided in all things by the law of Christ made man and by that of his Church and of his ministers, in a human visible manner, and by these means heal our spiritual weaknesses and our ignorance, since in these we shall find healing in abundance. If we forsake this path we are guilty not only of curiosity but presumption; nothing is to be believed on a supernatural level save that which is contained in the teaching of Christ made man, as I have said, and those of his ministers. St Paul went so far as to say: '*Quod si angelus de coelo evangelizaverit, praeterquam quod evangelizavimus vobis anathema sit*: If an angel from heaven preach any gospel to you other than that which we preach let him be anathema.'

A.M.C. II XXII vii

The Way, the Truth, the Life . . .

I wish I could convince those leading the spiritual life that the path to God does not consist in a multiplicity of meditations nor in ways and methods of making such nor in consolations, though these, as far as they go, may be necessary for beginners. The one thing needful is to be able to deny oneself truly in things both without and within, to give oneself for Christ's sake to suffering and total annihilation. For he who so denies himself will attain this suffering and annihilation and more besides; and likewise will find therein more than suffering. If a person be lacking in this, which is the sum and the root of the virtues, all else amounts to no more than roaming round in a maze and is no profit whatever, even though his meditations and communications be as celestial as those of the angels. Progress comes only through the imitation of Christ, the Way, the Truth and the Life. No man comes to the Father but by him, even as he says through St John the Evangelist. And elsewhere he says: 'I am the door; if any man enter by me he shall be saved.' Therefore, in my opinion, anyone who would walk in spiritual sweetness and ease and would flee from the imitation of Christ is of no worth.

A.M.C. II VII viii

PRAYER

The Paternoster ...

When his disciples begged Christ to teach them to pray, he told them all that is needful if the Eternal Father is to hear us – so well did he know his Father's nature. And yet he simply taught them the Paternoster with its seven petitions which comprise all our wants, spiritual and temporal : he did not teach them any other prayers, verbal or ceremonial. On the contrary, he told them that when they prayed they ought not to speak at length, since our heavenly Father knows what is best for us. This only he urged with great insistence that we should, persevere in prayer (that is, in the prayer of the Paternoster) saying : 'We ought at all times to pray without ceasing.' He did not, however, teach a variety of petitions, but rather that we should repeat our petitions frequently, with fervour and care. For, as I have said, in them is contained all the will of the Father and all that is for our good. Therefore when our Lord approached the eternal Father on three occasions, on all three he prayed in the words of the Paternoster, the Evangelist tells us, saying : 'Father, if I must needs drink this cup, may your will be done.' Also the ways in which he taught us to pray are two only. Either we are to pray in the quiet of our room, where without noise or distraction we can do so with unsullied heart : 'When you pray, go into your room, shut the door, and pray.' Or else, he taught that, we should go to a lonely, solitary place, as he himself used to, in the stillness of the night. And so there is no need to assign a fixed time or particular days or to set aside one time more than another . . . Nor need we resort to unusual forms of address or ambiguous phrases, but those only which the Church uses; for all are contained in the prayer we have mentioned: the Paternoster.

A.M.C. III XLIV iv

Contemplative prayer

The further the soul advances in the spiritual life the more does it cease from the operation of the faculties in isolated acts, for it becomes occupied more and more in one act that is comprehensive and pure; and so the faculties, which were moving towards a destination where the soul has already arrived, cease to function, just as feet cease to move when a journey is ended. If all were movement, we would not arrive. And if all things were means, where or when would we have our pleasure in the end — in the goal?

A.M.C. II XII vi

When the spiritual person cannot meditate let him learn to be quiet in God, fastening his loving attention on him, his understanding at rest — even though he may think he is doing nothing. For thus gradually (and quickly, too) divine tranquillity and peace will be infused into the soul, along with a wonderful, sublime knowledge of God, enfolded in divine love. And let him not meddle in forms, meditations and images or any kind of reflection, for fear the soul be disturbed and brought out of its contentment and tranquillity, which will result only in a feeling of distaste and repugnance. And if a person has scruples that he is doing nothing, he should reflect that he is doing no small thing in calming the soul and bestowing upon it quiet and tranquillity unaccompanied by any act or desire. This Our Lord asks through David: *'Vacate et videte quoniam ego sum Deus*: Learn to be empty of all things [within and without] and you will see that I am God.'

A.M.C. II XV v

A ray of darkness . . .

The clearer and more manifest are the things of God in themselves, the darker and more hidden are they on the natural level; just as the stronger the light, the more power it has to dazzle, indeed blind, the eyes of the owl; and the more directly we gaze upon the sun, the deeper is the darkness with which it blots out our vision, overcoming and overwhelming it by reason of its weakness.

Likewise when the divine light of contemplation is directed upon the soul which is not yet fully enlightened, this causes within it a spiritual darkness. For it not only overcomes the soul, but overwhelms and darkens the functioning of its natural intelligence. Hence St Dionysius and other mystical theologians call this infused contemplation a ray of darkness – for the soul, that is to say, which is not enlightened and purged – since the natural power of the intellect is surpassed and overwhelmed by this supernatural light. And so David says, 'Near to God and round him are darkness and cloud.' This is not, in fact, so, but it seems so to our weakened understanding, dazzled and darkened as it is by a light of such power.

D.N.S. II V iii

The ladder of contemplation

This ladder of contemplation, which comes down from God, is foreshadowed by the ladder which Jacob saw in his sleep, on which angels were ascending and descending between God and man, and man and God who was himself at the top of the ladder. All this, the Scriptures say, happened at night, while Jacob slept, so that this road, this ascent to God, is secret.

D.N.S. II XVIII iv

Contemplation is first and foremost – and this is why it is called a ladder – the science of love. It is an infused, loving knowledge of God: it illumines the soul and, enkindling it with love, lifts it step by step to God, its creator. For love alone is able to unite the soul to God.

D.N.S. II XVIII v

Even as a ladder has steps that we may go up, it has them also that we may come down. Of a like nature is secret contemplation. For while it raises the soul to God, it humbles it in respect of self. Intimations that come to us from God humble the soul, yet at the same time exalt it. For on this path the way down is the way up and the way up is the way down, for he who humbles himself is exalted and he who exalts himself is humbled. Moreover God makes the soul go up this ladder that it may come down and he makes it come down that it may go up, that the words of the Wise Man be fulfilled : 'Before the soul is exalted it is humbled, and before it is humbled it is exalted.'

D.N.S. II XVIII ii

Peace of soul . . .

Disquiet occasioned by adverse circumstances is of no avail. Indeed it makes things worse and harms even the soul. And so David said : 'In truth it is vain for a man to be disquieted.' For it is obvious that to disquiet oneself is vain, since it benefits no one. If everything, therefore, were to come to an end and be annihilated, if all things were to go wrong and turn to adversity, it would be vain to be disquieted, for this brings hurt, not relief. On the other hand to bear all with calm and tranquillity not only brings the advantage of many blessings, but, in the midst of adversity, enables one to reach a clearer judgment and therefore to find a solution. Solomon, well acquainted with adversity and its solutions, said : 'I learnt that there is nothing better for a man than to rejoice and to do good in his life.'

A.M.C. III VI iii-iv

The power of love

Such is the overwhelming power and superabundance of love that Mary Magdalene, though she knew her Beloved was enclosed in the tomb by an immense sealed stone and surrounded by guards – so that the disciples might not steal the body – let none of these considerations stand in the way, but went with unguents before daybreak to anoint him.

D.N.S. II XIII vi

Love for our neighbour

The deeper our love for God, the deeper is our love for our neighbour. For when love is rooted in God the reason for all love is one and the same, the cause of all love one and the same.

A.M.C. III XXIII i

The poor in spirit . . .

I knew someone who for over ten years used a cross roughly made from a blessed palm, fastened with a pin bent round it. He did not cease to use it and even carried it with him until I took it away from him : this was someone with considerable sense and understanding. And I saw another who, when saying his prayers, used beads made of bones from the spine of a fish : his devotion was no less precious in the sight of God – it did not derive from workmanship or value.

D.N.S. I III ii

Not to impede the All

> When you think about anything,
> You cease to cast yourself upon the All.
> For to pass from the all to the All
> You have to deny yourself wholly in all.
> And when you come to possess it wholly,
> You must possess it without desiring anything.
> For, if you will have anything in all,
> Your treasure is not solely in God.

A.M.C. I XIII xii

Unless a man be born again . . .

'*Qui non ex sanguinibus neque ex voluntate carnis neque ex voluntate viri sed ex Deo nati sunt.*' God, St John the

Evangelist tells us, gave power to be sons of God – that is, to be transformed in God – only to those who are born not of blood (that is, of natural constitution and temperament) nor of the will of the flesh (that is, free will in accordance with our natural capacity and ability), still less of the will of man, wherein is included every form of judgment and comprehension that belongs to the understanding. No, he gave to none of these the power to become the sons of God. He gave it only to those who are born of God – to those, that is, who, born again through grace and dying to all that belongs to unregenerate man, are raised above themselves to the supernatural and receive from God this new birth and adoption which transcends anything we can imagine. As St John said: *'Nisi quis renatus fuerit ex aqua et Spiritu Sancto, non potest videre regnum Dei.* Unless a man be born again of water and the Holy Spirit, he cannot see the kingdom of God.' And to be born again in the Holy Spirit, in this life, is to have a soul most like God in perfection, having in it no stain of imperfection, so that a pure transformation may be fashioned in it through participation in union – though not in essence.

To understand more clearly let us make a comparison. A beam of sunlight falls upon a window-pane. If the pane is at all soiled or clouded, the beam will not be able to illumine it totally and transform it into its own light, as it would if the glass were without stain. However, the beam will illumine it to a lesser extent, depending upon how clean the pane is and this again will depend not on the beam of sunlight, but on itself – so much so that if the glass be wholly without stain the beam of sunlight will transform it and illumine it in such a manner that the pane will itself seem to be a beam of sunlight and will give the same light as the beam.

A.M.C. II V v-vi

Transformed in God through love ...

God dwells in and is substantially present in every soul, even the greatest of sinners. This kind of union is ever fashioned between God and creatures, whereby he preserves their being, so that if there were not this union they would at once be annihilated and cease to be. When, therefore, we speak of the union of the soul with God we are not speaking of this ever-present substantial union between God and creatures, but of the union and the transformation of the soul with God through love – which is something that is not continually present, but only when there is that likeness that comes through love. We shall call this the 'union of likeness', even as we call that other the 'union through substance or essence'. The former is natural, the latter supernatural. Moreover the latter exists when the two wills – that is, the will of the soul and the will of God – conform and there is nothing in one that is repellent to the other. Thus, when the soul frees itself wholly from that which is contrary to God's will and does not conform with it, this soul is transformed in God through love.

A.M.C. II V iii

If the blind lead the blind . . .

When the soul is at the mercy of its desires, it becomes
blind; for it is as if one who sees were guided by one
who does not see, which is the same as if both were blind.
In St Matthew Our Lord tells us: *'Si caecus caeco
ducatum praestet, ambo in foveam cadunt*: If the blind
lead the blind both fall into a ditch.' Again, what use
are eyes to a moth, since, attracted by the brightness of
a light, it is dazzled and lured into the flame? And again,
one who feeds upon desires is like a fish that is blinded
by a light which serves as darkness, preventing the
creature from seeing the trap which the fishermen are
preparing.

A.M.C. I VIII iii

Desires . . .

Just as smudges of soot mar a beautiful, flawless countenance, so desires can defile a soul that in itself is a
beautiful, perfect likeness of God.

A.M.C. I IX i

Desires weaken the strength of the soul: they are like
shoots that spring up at the foot of a tree, taking from it
the strength which enables it to bear fruit.

A.M.C. I X ii

It is the same whether a bird is held by a fine string or a stout one. In either case the bird is a prisoner if it does not snap the string and fly away.

A.M.C. I XI iv

The desires and attachment felt by the soul have as much power as, they say, has the sucking-fish when clinging to a vessel. For though this creature is small, if it gets a grip, the ship is unable to reach harbour or sail ahead.

ibid.

When the will is attached to one thing, a man prizes this beyond all others; although something else may be much better, he takes less pleasure in it. And if he wants to take pleasure in both, he inevitably does injustice to the more important, since he makes an equality between the two.

A.M.C. I V v

Desires wear out and exhaust the soul. They are like restless, discontented children who, perpetually demanding this or that from their mother, are never satisfied.

A.M.C. I VI vi

SPIRITUAL AVARICE

Misuse of statues

There are those who are less concerned with what a statue represents than with its craftsmanship and monetary value.

A.M.C. III XXXV iii

We need only think of the loathsome custom, prevalent today, whereby, far from rejecting the trappings of the world, some, solely to satisfy their own pleasure and vanity, dress up statues with the clothes devised by empty-headed persons . . . In this way genuine, serious devotion, which rejects and spurns vanity in any shape or form, deteriorates into little more than dressing up dolls!

A.M.C. III XXXV iv

The person who is truly devout consecrates, primarily, on the invisible; he needs few statues, uses few, and chooses those that are in keeping with the divine rather than the human, clothing them and himself in the garments of the world to come, following its fashions rather than those of this world . . . Nor is his heart attached to these statues; if they are taken away, he is not unduly disturbed, for he seeks within himself a living image of Christ crucified, for whose sake he desires, rather, that all be taken from him and he be left with nothing.

A.M.C. III XXXV v

Some persons, laden with wealth, good works and spiritual practices as well as virtues and favours granted by God – like vessels laden with treasure – make no progress nor come to harbour, because they have not the courage to break with some whim, attachment or affection (call it which you will). Yet all they have to do is to set sail resolutely, cut the ship's cable, or rid themselves of the clinging, sucking-fish of desire.

A.M.C. I XI iv

Many beginners display at times great spiritual avarice. Discontented with the spirituality granted them by God they are disconsolate and querulous because they do not derive from things spiritual the consolation they would like. Many are satiated with listening to advice and acquiring and reading books that treat of such matters. Indeed they spend on such things time that would be better spent on self-denial and acquiring a spirit of poverty. They weigh themselves down with statues and rosaries that are unusual in workmanship and costly. They discard one, take up another. Now it is one thing, now something different. Now they want this, now that, prefering a particular kind of cross, because it is unusual. Others you see adorned with *agnus dei*'s, relics, medals, like children with trinkets. I utterly condemn this concern with kind, number and workmanship : it is entirely contrary to poverty of spirit . . . True devotion must come from the heart.

D.N.S. I III i

Pilgrimages . . .

Someone intending to make a pilgrimage would do well to make it when others are not doing the same – even if the season is an unusual one. If there is a great crowd I would advise against going. People generally return from these pilgrimages in a state of greater distraction than when they set out. Many go for a change of air, not out of devotion.

A.M.C. III XXXVI iii

Spiritual malaise

When the pleasure they have found in spiritual things fades, some persons become embittered and bear with bad grace the aridity they suffer. This affects all they do. They become easily irritable – indeed, everyone finds them intolerable.

D.N.S. I V i

Others, annoyed by the misdemeanours of their neighbours, keep an uneasy watch over them. They even reproach them in anger, setting themselves up as paragons of virtue.

D.N.S. I V ii

Others, annoyed with themselves at their own failings, display an impatience that is utterly remote from humility. Indeed so impatient are they that they want to become saints in a day!

D.N.S. I V iii

Stillness . . .

What we must do in the dark night is leave the soul free and unencumbered, at rest from knowledge and thought. We must not trouble as to what to think or on what to meditate – be content, rather, to wait upon God peacefully, attentively, without anxiety, not straining to experience or perceive him. Such efforts only disquiet the tranquillity granted to the soul in contemplation.

D.N.S. I X iv

Rejoice
'I knew that there was nothing better for man than to rejoice and do good in his life.' By these words Solomon meant that in everything that befalls us, though it be

adverse, we should rejoice rather than be troubled, that we may not lose a blessing greater than any prosperity – tranquillity and peace of mind in all things which, whether they bring adversity or felicity, should be borne in the same manner.

A.M.C. III VI iv

Liberty of soul . . .

He will find liberty of soul, clarity of mind, rest, tranquillity, a peaceful confidence in God, a true reverence and worship of God which is rooted in the will . . . Attachment fosters anxiety which, like a bond, ties the spirit down to earth, allowing no enlargement of heart. Detachment, on the other hand, enables a person to have a clear understanding of things, so that he can grasp the truth relating to them, both naturally and supernaturally. Consequently he will enjoy them in quite a different way from one who is attached to them : he will have an advantage and superiority over such a one.

A.M.C. III XX ii

This man, then, has joy in all things – since his joy is dependent on none of them – just as though he possessed them all. In contrast, he who looks upon them in a spirit of ownership loses the pleasure they offer. The former, having his heart set on none of them, possesses them all, as St Paul says, in perfect freedom. The latter, because his will seeks domination over them, neither has nor can have possession of them. It is they that have enslaved his heart, so that he has become, as it were, a sorrowful captive.

A.M.C. III XX iii

Exaggerated penance

We should deplore the folly of those who burden themselves with outlandish penances and many other self-appointed practices, supposing this or that will be enough to bring them to the union of divine wisdom. For this is not so, unless they do their utmost to mortify their desires. If they troubled to bestow half their efforts on this they would advance further in a month than, by means of all the other practices, in many years. For just as we must till the earth if it is to bear fruit and not merely weeds, so we must mortify our desires if the soul is to advance. Otherwise, I venture to say, the soul, however great its efforts, does not advance on the road to perfection and the knowledge of God and of self any more than does seed grow when scattered on untilled ground.

A.M.C. I VIII iv

To arrive . . .

> To arrive at having pleasure in everything
> Desire to have pleasure in nothing.
> To arrive at possessing everything

Desire to possess nothing.

    To arrive at being everything

Desire to be nothing.

    To arrive at knowing everything

Desire to know nothing.

    To arrive at that in which you have no pleasure

Go by a way in which you have no pleasure.

    To arrive at that which you know not

Go by a way you know not.

    To arrive at that which you possess not

Go by a way that you possess not.

    To arrive at that which you are not

Go through that which you are not.

A.M.C. I XIII xi

THE SPIRITUAL CANTICLE

Song between the Soul and the Bridegroom

> *Bride*
> Where do you hide,
> My love, to leave me thus to sigh,
> When like a stag you stride
> Away from me who wounded lie?
> I followed, called your name, but saw you fly.
>
> You, shepherds, climbing high
> To the sheepfold on the hill above,
> If on your journey you descry
> Him there, then tell my love
> That now I sicken, faint and die.
>
> To search till love be found
> I'll make my way by river bank or hillside near,
> Nor pluck those flowers that here abound
> Nor animals give pause to fear,
> But seek to cross all frontiers, fortress-bound.

To the Creatures
Oh thickets dark to sight
Which he has planted with his loving care,
Oh fields of emerald, bright
With blossom, tell me fair
Did he but pass you ever in his flight?

The Creatures reply
He poured his graces wide
As through the groves his journey sped
And all with wonder eyed,
So where his glances spread
Each thing he saw was beautified.

Bride
Oh who can ease my pain?
Now yield to me at last what I desire,
And let me now arraign
All those who still conspire
To bear these other tidings I disdain.

And those who loiter near
Retail your beauty, more to grieve my heart,
And in their babblings I hear
Of ecstasies you did impart
That make me prostrate fall and death appear.

How can you still conceive
To live when parted from this living fire?
Even the arrows you receive

74

Were made from his desire
That in your love he did perceive.

Why did you pierce my heart,
And do not try and heal the pain?
Draw like a thief apart,
And steal from me again
To leave the plunder and depart.

Yet quench my fury now I plead,
For no one else but you can be my aid,
And let my eyes concede
To you who in them is portrayed:
Apart from you no other light I need.

Disclose to me your lovely face,
Destroy me wholly with its strange allure;
The pain my wonder does encase
In love can find no cure
But only in the presence of your grace.

Oh stream of crystal light,
Let on your surface soon appear
And suddenly grow bright
Those eyes which are so near
They dazzle still my inner sight.

My love, hide now your light,
I am in flight.

The Bridegroom
>   Sweep, my dove, and alight,
The wounded stag is nigh
And seen upon the height,
Cooled by your wings of airy flight.

The Bride
My Beloved is the mountain peak,
The valleys set with all their lonely trees,
The islands that with strangeness speak,
The streams that sing in mysteries,
The breeze's whisper, such as all the love-lorn seek.

This is the dark, a peace
All hushed before the breaking of the light,
The music when all voices cease,
The solitude in all its echoes bright,
The banquet that for each is love's increase.

Now blossoms here the bridal bed
With dens of lions that all around are laid,
The curtain set with purple thread,
In peace, its fabric, surely made,
And with a thousand golden shields outspread.

To find your footprints sure
The young girls trace their faint outline,
Drawn by the cynosure
To where the adored wine
Is thus transfigured to a balm divine.

The wine vault hidden deep
That is my lover's heart, now full I drink,
And then my path to overleap
Insensible into myself I sink,
Abandoning the flock that once I used to keep.

Here in his breast I did reside,
And sweet to savour was the art he taught.
I gave myself and nothing modified,
Nor from him ever withheld aught,
And promised I would always be his bride.

I shall instruct my soul
To serve him in its fullest opulence,
No other flock shall I control;
To love him with all diligence
Shall be for me my duty and my only goal.

If from this moment sure
I can no more with other men be found,
Say that I them abjure,
For now I tread a lover's ground
And being once lost, am held now most secure.

Some flowers and emeralds bright
When gathered in the dawn and glimmering with dew,
Green-garlanded with light,
A flower like you,
I'll bind and with one hair unite.

For see, that single hair,
That you so wondered at and prize
Upon my head, can bear
To hold you, and my eyes
Can thus all wounds of yours ensnare.

When first you gazed
Upon me, then your grace so filled my eyes
That they were dazed,
And you began to tantalise,
And I adored what in your own now blazed.

Do not my life despise
Nor let my swarthy looks repel,
When you these faults apprise
Your gaze will them dispel,
In grace and beauty my soul vitalise.

All foxes from hence drive
Because our vine is now in flower;
A bouquet we'll contrive
As from the roses' bower,
And no one on our mountain will arrive.

Fall, then, you icy gale,
And come, sweet zephyr, love's recall,
Within this orchard trail
Those perfumes that enthral;
My lover, brousing, will their scent inhale.

Bridegroom
And now the bride arrayed
Into the loving garden here is led,
And in its shade
She rests her head
Against her lover's arms and there is stayed.

Beneath the apple tree
You came at once to be my bride,
And plighted then your troth to me :
This place you purified
Where once your mother, violated, lay in misery.

You birds with sweeping flight,
Lions, stags and fallow-deer who leap in play,
Mountains and valleys, rivers bright,
Waters and winds who joys display,
And all that guard and haunt the fearful night :

By the trembling of the lute
And the songs and canticles the sirens hymned,
I conjure you be mute,
With all your echoes dimmed :
My bride must sleep, her rest be absolute.

Bride
Oh maidens of Judea,
Now while the flowers and roses still retain
The perfumes of ambrosia,
Live in the outer plain

And do not seek to cross our threshold here.

Now hide yourself, my love, awhile,
And gaze across the distant mountain view,
Keep silent while
You watch her retinue
Who voyage to that far and secret isle.

Bridegroom
That dove, all silvery-white,
The Ark rejoins, the leaf returns :
She stays her flight
When she her mate discerns
Where the green river is in sight.

In solitude she lonely waits,
And in this solitude she builds her nest :
In solitude he animates
The beloved one at his behest;
This solitude the wound that love creates.

Bride
My love, let us both thrill
To all your beauty so enhances –
The mountains and the hill,
The stream in all its dances;
Let us both seek the woods, be secret still.

And soon we shall abide
Upon that hill with all its caverns dark,
And here we both can hide

80

Where we shall leave no mark,
And with the juice of pomegranates each be vivified.

And there from you I'll know
Your truth, for which my soul has long aspired,
And there on me bestow
That which my heart has so desired,
The truth I learned so short a while ago.

The whisper of the breeze again,
The songs, that are so lingering sweet, of Philomel,
The groves, your elegant demense,
The night's soft knell
That tells of fire that burns but does not pain.

While no one was attending
Aminadab has all withdrawn his forces;
The siege has found its ending,
And teams of horses
Distantly are seen to the waters now descending.

The Holy Spirit speaking within us . . .

The Holy Spirit, who supports our weakness, dwells within us, as St Paul says, and, with groanings which cannot be uttered, intercedes for us, pleading for that which we cannot sufficiently grasp or understand so as to express it ourselves. For who can write down what the Spirit reveals to loving souls in whom he dwells?

Who can put into words the feelings with which he inspires them? Finally who can say what it is he makes them desire? Absolutely no one, not even those souls through whom he passes. That is why, through imagery, comparisons and similitudes, they allow something of what they feel to overflow. That is why they utter mystical secrets from the abundance of the spirit rather than explain rationally. If these similitudes are not read with the simplicity of love and understanding which is embodied in them, they make nonsense rather than provide a rational explanation, as we see to be the case with the *Song of Songs* and other books contained in Scripture, where, since the Holy Spirit cannot convey his wealth of meaning in the language of everyday speech, he has resort to strange imagery and similitudes used by mystics. Hence learned doctors, despite all they have said and yet may say, cannot find words to expound fully these things nor indeed can they be expounded in any words whatsoever. What is expounded, therefore, is a minimum of the content.

As these stanzas, then, have been inspired by a love which is the fruit of a rich mystical experience, they cannot be adequately expounded nor shall I attempt so to expound them – only to shed some light in a general way. This, I think, is best, for sayings prompted by love are better left in their entirety so that each reader can avail himself of them in his own way, according to his own measure rather than pruned down to an interpretation which not everyone will find acceptable. And so, although the stanzas are expounded to a certain extent, there is no reason for anyone to be confined to this particular interpretation. For mystical wisdom which derives from love (and love is the theme of these stanzas) does not have to be understood on a rational level for it to engender love and affection in the soul. Like faith, it enables us to love God without our understanding him.

S.C. Prologue i-ii

The Lover lives in the Beloved, the Beloved in the Lover

Such likeness does love fashion in the transformation of the two who love each other that each, it may be said, is the other and the two are one. For the one makes a gift of self to the other : each gives and abandons self to the other. Thus each lives in the other and the one is the other and both are one through the transformation of love. Thus St Paul says: *'Vivo autem, iam non ego, vivit vero in me Christus:* I live, yet not I, but Christ in me.' He means that although he lives, his life is not his own, because he has been transformed into Christ, so that his life is divine rather than human.

According to this likeness of transformation, therefore, we can say that St Paul's life and the life of Christ are one in union of love which, in heaven, will be perfected in the divine life for all who merit being in God; for, transformed in God they will live the life of God, not their own, and yet it will be their own, for the life of God will be theirs. Then they will say truly : 'We live, yet not we ourselves, for God lives in us.' This may happen here on earth, as it did to St Paul. It will not, however, happen in a complete, perfect manner, although the soul may reach a transformation of love as in the spiritual marriage, which is the highest state attainable in this life – for everything can be looked upon as an outline of love, as compared with that perfect image of transformation in glory. But when this outline is attained during life on earth, it is indeed a great happiness because the Loved one is well pleased. Hence, desiring that the Bride should engrave him upon her heart, he says to her in the *Song of Songs:* 'Set me as a seal upon your heart, as a seal upon your arm.'

S.C. XI vi & vii

A hidden God

The soul enamoured of the Word, the Son of God, her Loved One, longing to be united to him through a clear, essential vision, tells of the anxiety engendered by her love, reproaches him for his absence – the more so because, wounded by the love for which she has abandoned all else, even her very self, she still suffers the absence of him whom she loves and, being not yet loosed from mortal flesh, cannot have fruition of him in the glory of eternity. And so she asks: 'Where do you hide?' as though she were saying: 'O Word, my Loved One, show me where you hide' thus begging him to reveal his divine essence. For the place where the Son of God is hidden as, St John the Evangelist says, is the bosom of the Father, which is the divine essence, remote and hidden from mortal eye and understanding. Thus Isaiah: 'In truth you are a God who hides yourself.' And be it noted that however sublime are the communications between the soul and God in this life and likewise the revelations of His presence, however lofty and exalted is the knowledge of him, these are not God in his essence nor have they any relation to him. He is truly hidden from the soul and in all these manifestations the soul should think of him as hidden, seek him as hidden, saying: 'Where do you hide?' For neither is a sublime communication of him nor a revelation of his presence by way of the senses a clear testimony of his presence nor is aridity or the lack of these things a less clear testimony. Hence the prophet Job: *'Si venerit ad me non videbo eum; et si abierit, non intelligam:* If he [that is God] comes to me, I shall not see him; and if he goes away I shall not understand him.' This means that should the soul experience any special communication or knowledge of God or any other such feeling, it must not therefore believe that it possesses God more completely or is itself more deeply in God, nor – however profound such an experience may be – must it suppose that what it feels and understands is God in his essence. And if all these communications which come by way of the senses and the intelligence fail, it must not, for that reason, conclude that God is failing it.

S.C. I i-ii

The wounds of love

The healing of the wounds of love comes only from him who inflicted the wounds. Hence, the soul says that she went forth calling for him who dealt the wound, begging to be healed, crying out at the violence of the burning caused by the wound.

S.C. I xi

Whosoever goes about in affliction for God, he has surrendered himself to God and God loves him.

S.C. I xii

It is of the nature of perfect love to refuse to accept or take anything for oneself, or to attribute anything to oneself. All things are for the Beloved.

S.C. XXIII i

The soul that longs for God is not consoled or satisfied by any other company whatsoever : all else makes and causes within it an ever-increasing solitude, until it finds him.

S.C. XXXIV ii

To reveal one's need is enough . . .

One who loves with discretion does not beg for what he lacks and desires. He merely reveals his need, so that the Beloved may do as seems good to him. At the wedding in Cana of Galilee the Blessed Virgin spoke to her beloved Son, not openly imploring him for wine, but saying: 'They have no wine.' Moreover the sisters of Lazarus sent to Christ not to ask to heal their brother, but to tell him to take note how he whom he loved was sick.

S.C. II viii

Creatures . . .

On the earth are countless varieties of animals and plants; in the water countless kinds of fish; in the air a great diversity of birds; moreover the element of fire animates and conserves them all. Thus each kind of creature dwells in its element, is set and planted there as in its own wood, the place in which it is born and nurtured. In truth so God commanded when he created the world. He commanded the earth to bring forth plants and animals; the sea and water, fish, the air, to be the dwelling of birds. Therefore, the soul realising that so he commanded and so it was done, says: 'Planted with his loving care.'

S.C. IV ii

The soul says deliberately, 'with his loving care'. For although God did many things by the hand of others, whether angels or men, the act of creation was something he did himself, by his own hand. And so the soul, when reflecting upon what he did with his own hand, cannot but love God, the Loved One.

S.C. IV iii

The Grove . . .

By the grove is meant God, along with all the creatures that are in him : for just as all the trees and plants have their life and roots in the grove, so the creatures, celestial and terrestrial, have their roots and life in God. Hence the soul says that there she will show herself to God, seeing that he is life and being to all creatures, since she knows that in him are their beginning and duration, for without him nothing is granted to the soul nor does she consider herself able to know them in the spiritual manner. Also, the soul longs to see the beauty of the grove; that is, the grace and wisdom and beauty which not only does each of the creatures receive from God, but which they enjoy among themselves in a wise, ordered and mutual inter-relationship of both the higher creatures and the lower. This is to know the creatures in the manner of contemplation, which is a source of great joy, for it is to have knowledge concerning God.

S.C. XXXVIII viii

Traces of God's image . . .

God created all things without difficulty or hindrance, bestowing upon them some trace of himself.

S.C. V i

The creatures are, as it were, traces of God's passing, wherein he reveals his might, power, wisdom and other divine qualities.

S.C. V iii

The Son, St Paul tells us, is the brightness of God's glory, the image of his substance. Let it be understood, then, that God looked upon all things in this image of his Son alone, which was to give them their natural being, bestow upon them diverse natural gifts and graces, make them complete and perfect, even as he says in Genesis: 'God saw all the things he had made and they were good.' To see them and find them good was to make them good in the Word, his Son. And not only did he bestow upon them their being and their natural graces, when, as we have said, he looked upon them, but also in this image of his Son alone he left them clothed in beauty, bestowing upon them supernatural being. For when the Word became flesh he exalted man in the beauty of God and therefore exalted all creatures in him, since in uniting himself with man he united himself with the nature of them all. Hence the Son of God said: *'Si ego exaltatus fuero a terra, omnia traham ad me ipsum:* If I be lifted up I will draw all things unto me.' And so in this lifting up through the Incarnation of his Son and in the glory of his Resurrection according to the flesh, not only did the Father beautify the creatures in part, but left them, we can say, clothed with beauty and dignity.

S.C. V iv

Messenger and Message . . .

Nothing, Lord, on earth or in heaven can give to the soul the knowledge of you it desires to have. None can tell me what I want to know. You, therefore, be yourself both messenger and message.

S.C. VI vi

He who has fallen in love . . .

The more the angels inspire me, Lord, and the more men tell me about you, the more they make me love you.

S.C. VII viii

Let me see you face to face with the eyes of my soul!

S.C. X iv

He who has fallen in love has been robbed, or reft as they say, of his heart by the one whom he loves. For his heart strays far from him, set upon his beloved. And so he has no heart of his own, for it belongs to the one whom he loves. And so the soul can know whether or not it loves God: if it loves him it will have no heart save for God only.

S.C. IX iv

As long as the heart does not truly possess that which it loves, it must needs be weary until it attains possession; for it is like an empty vessel waiting to be filled; a hungry man longing for food; an invalid sighing for health; one who, suspended in the air, can find no foothold.

S.C. IX v

Like to the hart . . .

The Bridegroom likens himself to a hart. Now, the hart as is well known, mounts to lofty places and, when

91

wounded, seeks in all haste refreshment in cool waters. Moreover if it hears his mate complain and sees she is wounded he immediately goes to her, caresses and fondles her. Even so the Bridegroom, seeing the Bride wounded with love for him, comes when she sighs, wounded likewise with love for her; for when two love each other the wound of one is the wound of both.

S.C. XII viii

Philomel . . .

Even as the song of Philomel, the nightingale, is heard in the spring, when the cold and the rains of winter all have passed, making music to charm the ear and refresh the spirit, even so in this sharing and transformation of love the Bride is sheltered and freed from all terrestrial change and turbulence and detached and cleansed from imperfections, defects and flaws. She feels within her the freshness of spring, in which she hears the voice of her Bridegroom, her Philomel, gladdening and renewing her spirit saying, 'Rise, make haste, my Beloved, my dove, my beautiful one. Come, for the winter is past, the rains are gone far away, the flowers appear on the earth, the time for pruning is come and the voice of the turtle-dove is heard in our land.'

S.C. XXXVIII vi

The turtle-dove . . .

The Bridegroom calls the soul a turtle-dove. That this
be better understood, when the turtle-dove, it is written,
cannot find its mate, it neither perches on a green bough
nor drinks fresh cool water nor settles beneath the shade
nor joins the other birds. But once it is united with its
mate, then it finds pleasure in all these things.

S.C. **XXXIII** iv

The two become one . . .

As in the consummation of marriage according to the
flesh, the two become one, as the Scriptures say, so
when this spiritual marriage between God and the soul
is consummated there are two natures in one spirit and
love of God. Imagine the light of a star or a candle
merged into and united with that of the sun. The light
that shines is not that of the star or the candle : the
sun has absorbed the lesser lights into itself.

S.C. **XXVII** ii

My Beloved . . .

The mountains soar aloft : they are abundant, spacious,
lovely to look upon, graceful, fragrant with flowers.
These mountains my Beloved is to me.

S.C. **XIII, XIV** vi

The solitary valleys are peaceful, pleasant, cool, shady, watered by running streams. In the diversity of their trees, in the joyous song of birds, they refresh and delight the senses. In their solitude and silence they give rest. These valleys my Beloved is to me.

S.C. XIII, XIV vii

The strange islands are encircled by the sea, far away across the sea, withdrawn, remote from converse with men. On them are found and nurtured things other than those within our experience, strange in kind, their qualities unfamiliar to men. They awake exceeding wonder in those who see them. And thus, because of these great, wondrous marvels and this strange knowledge remote from the everyday knowledge granted to the soul, God is called 'strange islands'. Now there are two reasons for calling someone strange; either he lives withdrawn from men or he is outstanding and singular among others in his actions and his works. For both these reasons the soul speaks of God as 'strange'. Not only has he all the strangeness of islands that have not been seen, but likewise his ways, counsels and works are strange, unfamiliar and wondrous in the sight of men. Nor is it surprising if God is strange to those who have not seen him, since he is strange also to the holy angels and the souls who see him; for they cannot see him perfectly nor shall they so see him; until the day of judgment they will continually see in him so many things that are new, according to his profound judgments and his works of compassion and justice, that they will wonder continually and marvel for ever more. Wherefore angels and men alike can speak of him as 'strange islands'. Only to himself is he not strange, nor to himself is he new.

S.C. XIII, XIV viii

The north wind and the south wind . . .

The wind from the north is dry and icy, shrivelling the flowers. And because spiritual dryness has this effect upon the soul in which it dwells, the soul calls it 'north wind'. It is also called 'dead' because it quenches spiritual sweetness.

S.C. XXVI ii

The south wind is a gentle breeze which brings rain and causes grass and plants to grow, flowers to open and distil their fragrance. By this breeze, therefore, the soul denotes the Holy Spirit who, she says, awakens love.

S.C. XXVI iii

Anxiety . . .

Evil spirits, jealous of the recollection and tranquillity of the soul, awaken within feelings of anxiety, restlessness and fear. These the Bride calls 'foxes', for just as the shrewd, agile little foxes, bounding lithely, tear down and destroy the blossom in the vineyards at the season when they are in flower, so cunning, malicious spirits with no less speed disturb and distract the soul.

S.C.XXV ii

Fear not . . .

Multae tribulationes iustorum. Many are the tribulations of the righteous, but the Lord will rescue them from all these. The soul that truly loves, that values her Loved One above all things, that trusts in his love and favour, does not find it hard to say, 'Nor will I fear the wild beasts'.

S.C. III vii

A spring of living water . . .

Christ our Lord, speaking to the Samaritan woman, called faith a spring. Within those who believed in him he would, he said, make for himself a spring of water, gushing up unto life everlasting. And this water was the Spirit which those who believed in him would receive in faith.

S.C. XI ii

The Darkness of Contemplation . . .

Contemplation is dark and therefore is also called 'mystical theology', which means the secret, hidden wisdom of God, wherein, without the noise of words or the service and help of any bodily or spiritual sense, as in the silence and stillness of night, concealed by darkness from whatever is of the senses and nature, God teaches the soul in a deeply hidden, secret manner, without its knowing how this is so. Some spiritual persons call this: 'understanding yet not understanding.'

S.C. XXXVIII ix

Even as a sunbeam is dim and black to the eye of the bat, so the sublime, shining things of God are dark to our understanding.

S.C. XXXVIII x

The tranquil night of contemplation . . .

In the spiritual sleep in which the soul rests in the embrace of her Beloved, she possesses and finds joy in all the calm, tranquillity and stillness of the peaceful night and receives in God, along with this, a dark and profound intelligence bestowed on her by God. Hence, her Beloved, the Bride says, is to her the tranquil night.

S.C. XIII, XIV xxii

Yet this tranquil night, the soul says, is not the same as the dark night. Rather it resembles the night that is already nearing the dawn; for this calm repose in God is not total darkness to the soul, as is the dark night, but tranquillity and stillness experienced in the divine night, in a fresh knowledge of God in which the spirit, raised to the divine light, is quiet, tranquil. And the Bride fittingly calls the divine light the rising of the dawn, that is the morning; for even as the dawn dispels the darkness of night and reveals the light of day, so this spirit, at rest and at peace in God, is raised from the darkness of natural knowledge to the morning of a supernatural knowledge of God – not brightly, but, as we say, dimly, as when the dawn is rising; for the night at that time is neither wholly night nor wholly day, but like twilight (between two lights), so this God-given tranquillity and solitude is not flooded with divine light in all its brilliance, yet it does to some degree participate in it.

In this calm the understanding is aware of itself as raised aloft, in a manner beyond natural understanding, to the divine light, even as one who, after a long sleep, suddenly opens his eyes to the light of day. This knowledge, so I believe, is anticipated in David's words: *'Vigilavi et factus sum sicut passer solitarius in tecto:* I kept watch like a bird alone on a housetop.' It is as though he said, 'I opened the eyes of my understanding and found myself above every kind of natural knowledge, alone, on the housetop – that is, high above all things here below'. And he says he became like a bird that is alone, because in contemplation of such a kind the spirit has the properties of this bird. First, the bird perches on the highest place, even as the spirit in this state is engaged in the highest contemplation. Secondly, it keeps its beak windward, even as the spirit directs its affection towards the source from which comes the spirit of love, that is God. Thirdly, it is alone, not wanting another bird near it, so that if another perches at its side, it flies away. Even so the spirit in this state of contemplation is withdrawn from all things, detached from all, wanting only solitude in God. Fourthly, even as the bird sings sweetly, so does the spirit sing to God at this time, for the praise it sings to God tells of a love delectable to itself and precious in God's sight.

S.C. XIII, XIV xxiii–xxiv

Loving God in and through the Holy Spirit . . .

The soul seeing the reality of the boundless love with which God loves her, longs to love him no less sublimely, no less perfectly. Hence she desires to be transformed, because the soul can only attain this equality and completeness of love if its own will is wholly transformed into the will of God wherein the two wills are united in such a manner that they become one. And so there is equality of love for the will of the soul that is transformed into the will of God is then wholly God's will – the will of the soul is not lost, but has become the will of God. Thus the soul loves God with the will of God, which is also her will. And so she will love God as much as she is loved by God, since she loves him with the will of God himself, with the same love with which he loves her, that is in the Holy Spirit who is given to the soul, even as the Apostle says : *'Gratia Dei diffusa est in cordibus nostris per Spiritum Sanctum qui datus est nobis*. And so the soul loves God in the Holy Spirit, together with the Holy Spirit.'

S.C. XXXVII ii

3

THE LIVING FLAME OF LOVE

Love Song of the Soul in intimate union with God

Oh love with living flame
And with such tender skill
How deep you reach within my heart!
Now, since you cannot change again,
Conclude it, have your will
And rend its tissues all apart.

Oh cautery sublime!
Oh wound all my delight!
Oh tender hand! Oh touch how delicate still!
You give us life beyond all time
And of our debts you have made light!
You bring my death to life while yet you kill.

Oh lamps of a fiery clime
From whom all radiance glows
To the inner caverns of my sight,
Once blinded in its shadowy time,

Now, while this strange springtime blows,
You give to your own both heat and light.

What stillness, your love's gift,
You bring again to my poor heart
Which you your secret home may call :
In your breathings airy drift,
In joy and glory set apart,
How delicately in love you make me fall!

The flame of the Holy Spirit ...

This flame of love within the soul is the Spirit of the Bridegroom – that is the Holy Spirit. And the soul feels this flame within not only as a fire that has consumed and transformed it in wondrous love, but as a fire which, burning within, emits flames. Moreover the flame bathes the soul in glory and refreshes it with the temper of life eternal. And the operation of the Holy Spirit in the soul is such that it is transformed in love and his interior activity causes it to emit flames which are the enkindling of love wherein the will of the soul is united, and it loves most deeply, being made one with the flame of love. And these acts of love on the part of the soul are most precious. One of them alone is of greater merit, greater worth, than all the soul may have achieved in its life apart from this transformation, however much that be. As is the difference between a habit and an act so is that which exists between transformation in love and the flame of love. Compare a log of wood which has been set on fire and the flame which it emits – the flame is the effect of the fire that burns the wood.

L.F.L. I iii

The fire of union . . .

The Soul, therefore, that is in a state of transformation of love may be said, normally, to be like a log that is continually assailed by fire. The acts of the soul are the flame that arises from the fire of love. And the more intense is this fire of union, the more vehement is the flame issuing from it. And in this flame the acts of the will are united and soar aloft, borne away and absorbed into the flame of the Holy Spirit, even as the angel soared aloft to God in the flame of the sacrifice of Manoah. When this happens the soul indeed can perform no act of itself – only if the Holy Spirit so moves it, in which case whatsoever it does is divine, since it is impelled and moved by God.

L.F.L. I iv

God said that the Father, the Son and the Holy Spirit would come to him who loved him and would make their abode in him. This would come to pass, he said, by making such a one to dwell in the Father, the Son and the Holy Spirit, in the life of God.

L.F.L. Prologue ii

If it be your will . . .

'Perfect me now if it be your will.' Herein the soul makes
the two petitions which in St Matthew the Lord bids us
make : '*Adveniat regnum tuum. Fiat voluntas tua.* That
is : Grant me this kingdom in its perfection, according
to your will. Grant that this may come to pass.'

L.F.L. I xxiii

Words of life . . .

'Are not my words like fire?' the prophet Jeremiah
asked. God's words, he himself tells us through St John
the Evangelist, are spirit and life and are recognised by
those who have ears to hear; those who, as I say, are
untarnished and enkindled with love. But those whose
palate is not healthy and find pleasure in other things
cannot recognise the spirit and life contained in the
words. So, too, the loftier the words spoken by the Son
of God, the more they failed to please those whose
understanding was clouded. When the Lord taught the
beautiful, moving truth about the Holy Eucharist many
who heard him turned away.

L.F.L. I v

A short prayer penetrates the heavens.

L.F.L. I xxvii

God is a consuming fire . . .

Our Lord God is a consuming fire, a fire of love. This fire, infinite in power, can consume to a degree no man could measure, and, burning with this vehemence, can transform into itself whatever it touches.

L.F.L. II ii

It is a wonderful thing that though this fire has such vehemence, though it could consume a thousand worlds more easily than a natural fire could consume a handful of flax, it does not consume those within whom it burns nor does it destroy them. Rather, in proportion to its power and heat it gives them joy and unites them to God himself, burning gently within them by reason of the purity of their hearts. So it happened, we read in the Acts, when this fire came down with great vehemence and enkindled the Apostles. And, St Gregory says, the Apostles burned with an inner joy. And this is what the Church means by the words: 'There came from heaven fire, burning not, but giving forth a radiance, consuming not but giving light.' For since the purpose of these communications is to magnify the soul, this fire does not cause it distress, but rather enlarges it. Neither does it weary the soul, but causes it delight, making it glorious and enriched, for which reason the soul calls the fire beautiful.

L.F.L. II iii

Inadequate spiritual directors . . .

Such persons have no understanding of what spirituality means. They insult God and show him great irreverence, laying their clumsy hands on what he himself is fashioning. For at great cost to himself God has brought these followers of his where they are — in this solitude, this emptiness of their faculties and activities, so that he may speak to their hearts, which is what he desires to do. He has himself taken them by the hand. He himself reigns in their souls in an abundance of peace and tranquillity, causing their natural faculties, with which they toiled the night long and achieved nothing, to fail. He has brought them quiet without working upon the senses, since neither the senses nor any act emanating from them is capable of receiving the Spirit.

L.F.L. III xlvi

Not all the directors are wise enough to deal with all the contingencies, all the possibilities which they may encounter on the spiritual road, nor is their spirituality so flawless that they know in every condition how a soul should be guided and directed. . . . Not everyone who can hew a block of wood can carve a statue; not everyone who can carve a statue can give it outline and polish; not everyone who can polish it is able to paint it; not everyone who can paint it is able to give the finishing touches. Each person occupied in making a statue can do only that in which he is skilled; if he attempts more he destroys the work.

L.F.L. III xlix

Let the soul rest in the hands of God. Let it have trust in him, committing itself to neither the hands nor the working of others.

L.F.L. III lviii

The soul which has even one degree of love already abides in God who is its centre.

L.F.L. I xii

In this state of quiet, the soul, it should be borne in mind, though it may not be aware of making progress or indeed of doing anything, is achieving more than if it were walking on its own feet. For God is bearing it in his arms and so, although it is making progress in accordance with God's will, it is unaware of any movement. It is not, it is true, working with its own faculties but is accomplishing more than if it were doing so. Nor is it surprising that the soul should be unable to realise this: the senses cannot grasp the work that God is doing for, as the Wise Man says, 'The words of wisdom are heard in silence.'

L.F.L. III lviii

'Brightnesses' . . .

The soul experiences three main kinds of love which could be called 'brightnesses'. First, the soul now loves God not through itself but through God: this is a brightness of a wondrous nature since it loves through the Holy Spirit, even as the Father and the Son love one another, as the Son himself says in St John the Evangelist: 'May the love with which you have loved me, be in them and I in them.' The second 'brightness' is to love God in God; for in this intense union the soul is absorbed in the love of God and God surrenders himself to the soul with great intensity. The third 'brightness' is such that the soul loves God for who he is: it loves him not only because he is generous, good, glorious and the like in relation to itself, but much more earnestly because he is all these things in his essence.

L.F.L. III lxxii

We assume others are like ourselves . . .

Of such stuff are we that we think others are like ourselves. We judge others as we judge ourselves – so that our judgment takes its beginning from within self, not from without. Hence, the thief believes that others steal; he who is lustful that others are lustful; he who bears malice, that others bear malice, whereas his judgment in reality derives from his own malice. The good man thinks well of others, his judgment deriving from the goodness of his heart. So, again, he who is careless and idle thinks the same of others. Hence, when we ourselves are careless and idle in the sight of God we imagine it is God, not ourselves, who is guilty of these faults, as we read in the 43rd Psalm where David says to God: 'Arise, Lord, why do you sleep?' attributing to God qualities that are in man. For though it is man who has fallen asleep, we bid God arise and wake. And yet he who keeps Israel slumbers not.

L.F.L. IV viii

God within us . . .

When the King of Heaven has revealed himself to the soul as a friend, an equal, a brother, we have no longer cause to fear.

L.F.L. IV xiii

God dwells secretly in every soul: he is hidden in its very substance. Were this not so the soul could not exist.

L.F.L. IV xiv

Happy is he who is ever aware that God dwells within him, taking his rest within his heart.

Even in those who have not attained union, God nevertheless dwells secretly. Nor is he loath to do so, for they are, after all, enfolded in his grace, although as yet they are not ready for union.

L.F.L. IV xvi

I am yours . . .

He who loves another and does good to him, loves him and does good in accordance with his own attributes and powers. And so, since your Bridegroom, who is within you, is omnipotent, he bestows on you omnipotence and loves you therewith; and since he is wise, he loves you, you observe, with wisdom; since he is good, with goodness; since he is holy, with holiness; since he is righteous, with righteousness; since he is merciful with mercy; since he is compassionate and clement, with compassion and clemency; since his being is strong, sublime and of great delicacy, with strength, sublimity and delicacy; since he is clean and pure, with cleanliness and purity; since he is true, with truth. Moreover since he is generous, you see likewise that he loves you with generosity, without self-interest, and solely that he may confer blessings upon you. Again, as he is supreme humility, he loves you with supreme humility, and with the highest esteem, making himself an equal to you and making you equal to him, joyfully revealing in this way his countenance full of grace and saying to you : 'I am yours and I am for you; I delight in being as I am that I may give myself to you and be yours.'

L.F.L. III vi

An obstreperous soul . . .

Sometimes when God thinks fit to keep the soul in a state of quiet tranquillity, the latter, availing itself of its powers of mind and imagination persists in crying out and trying to walk. You have only to think of those children who, when their mothers are carrying them in their arms so that they may not have to walk, keep whimpering and striking out with their feet in their eagerness to walk – thus making progress impossible both for themselves and the mothers. Or think of an artist trying in vain to paint a portrait of someone who will not stay still for a moment.

The soul in this state must reflect that, although it is not conscious of making progress, it is making more than if it were walking on its feet : because God bears it in his arms it is not conscious of movement. It is not surprising that the soul is unaware of what is happening, for the senses cannot perceive the nature of God's work. The soul, therefore, should rest in the hands of God, have confidence in him and entrust itself neither to the hands nor the activities of others.

L.F.L. III lvii-lviii

If you open the shutters . . .

As the sun, when it rises in the morning and shines upon your house, will stream in if you open the shutters, so God, who keeps Israel and slumbers not, nor sleeps, will enter the soul that is empty and fill it with blessings.

L.F.L. III xl

God, like the sun, is above our souls, ready to stream into us. Spiritual directors, therefore, ought to be content to prepare the soul in accordance with evangelical perfection, which means our being detached and devoid of whatever is sinful. They should not go beyond this in building up the soul, for it is a work that belongs to God only, 'from whom comes down every perfect gift': 'For if the Lord build not the house, he who builds it labours in vain'; and in each soul, in a manner that seems good to him, God will build a supernatural dwelling place.

L.F.L. III xli

'The power of the Most High will overshadow you' . . .

To 'overshadow' is to cast a shadow. If someone casts his shadow upon another it means that he protects the other, grants him favours. When a shadow touches a person this means that he who overshadows him is at hand to befriend and protect. And so it is said to the Virgin that the power of the Most High will overshadow her, because the Holy Spirit is to approach so closely that he will come upon her. And be it noted that when something makes a shadow, this shadow matches it in nature and size. If something is cloudy and opaque it will make a dark, dense shadow. If it is clearer and lighter it will make a lighter shadow. Consider a log of wood and a crystal. The one being solid will make a dark shadow; the other being translucent a light one.

L.F.L. III xii

The brightness of the Father . . .

God is to the soul as are many lamps, each giving light in a distinctive way. From each the soul derives knowledge and from each receives the warmth of love in a particular manner. And yet all are, we may say, one; that is, all are one lamp – the Word which, St Paul says, is the brightness of the Father.

L.F.L. III iii

The touch of God . . .

Delicate touch! Word of God! Son of God! Through the delicacy of your divine being you subtly permeate the very substance of my soul. Touching it in its entirety yet delicately, you absorb it into yourself in a wondrous, supernatural way never heard of in the land of Canaan nor seen in Teman.

L.F.L. II xvii

My God! My life! Those whom you refine shall know you and behold you when you touch them: for purity responds to purity. You will touch them with the greater delicacy because you are hidden in the substance of their souls, which have been made beautiful and delicate. And, because they are withdrawn from creatures and all trace of creatures, you, Lord, conceal them in the hiding place of your presence, which is your divine Son, and you shelter them from the turmoil of mankind. Again, therefore, I say, Delicate touch! Touch most delicate, that with its strength causes the soul to melt and, allowing none else to touch it, makes it yours alone!

L.F.L. II xvii

In the joys of the spirit . . .

Those of you who seek to walk in security and comfort, if only you knew how needful it is to suffer and endure if you are to reach this sublime state – what benefit it is to suffer and be mortified so as to attain blessings so exalted! If you knew this, you would seek no consolation either from God or from aught else. Rather would you bear the Cross with vinegar and gall, counting this great happiness. For being thus dead to the world and to self, you would live in God in the joys of the spirit.

L.F.L. II xxiv

We have a dwelling with God in heaven . . .

Death is privation of life : when life comes there is left no trace of death. As to the Spirit, there are two kinds of life. One is beatific, which means seeing God face to face and must be preceded by the natural death of the body; as St Paul says, 'We know that if this our house of clay is dissolved, we have a dwelling with God in heaven.' The other is spiritual, which means possessing God in a union of love and is attained through the mortification of vices and desires, indeed of the soul's entire nature. Only through this purgation can the soul perfectly attain the spiritual life of union with God, even as the Apostle says, 'If you live according to the flesh you shall die; but if with the spirit you mortify the deeds of the flesh, you shall live.'

L.F.L. II xxviii

O death, I will be your death . . .

The soul, the true daughter of God that it now is, becomes wholly impelled by the Spirit of God; as St

Paul says, 'They that are moved by the Spirit of God are the sons of God.' Thus, as has been said, the understanding of the soul has become the understanding of God; its will, the will of God; its memory, the memory of God; its pleasure, the pleasure of God. Moreover the substance of this soul, though it cannot be the substance of God (its substance cannot be changed into this), is none the less united in God and absorbed into him and is thus God by participation in God, which comes about in this perfect life of the spirit, although not to the degree of perfection that the soul will attain in the next life . . . And so it is 'by slaying you have changed death into life.' For this reason the soul may say here on earth with St Paul: 'I live, yet not I but Christ in me.' Thus, the death of the soul is changed into the life of God, and the soul absorbed into life, since in it is likewise fulfilled the words of the Apostle: 'Death is absorbed in victory.' And the words of Hosea the prophet: 'O death, I will be your death, says the Lord.'

L.F.L. II xxx

Precious is the death of the righteous . . .

The death of those united to God is more beautiful, more moving than their entire life; for as they die they are aware of wondrous encounters and impulses of love. They resemble the swan which sings most sweetly when it is about to die – indeed on the very brink of death. Hence David says, 'Precious is the death of the righteous'; for at this time rivers of love flow forth from the soul to meet the sea — indeed so broad and so motionless are these rivers that they seem already to be the sea. The beginning and the end, the first and the last, merge into one to accompany the righteous man as he sets out, going forth to his kingdom. Praises are heard from the ends of the earth : this is the glory of the righteous.

L.F.L. I xxiv

PART THREE

Miscellanea

Excerpts from letters written by St John of the Cross

To M. Ana de San Alberto, Prioress of Caravaca
> Date uncertain.

Do not, I beg you, harbour foolish fears that make the soul cowardly. Give to God all he has given to you and gives you daily. You are trying to measure God, it seems to me, by the measure of your own capacity – you must not do this.

To M. Ana de San Alberto, Prioress of Caravaca
> Date uncertain.

How long do you imagine you are to be carried in the arms of others? I want to see you so detached, so independent, that not even hell could disturb you. Why these uncalled for tears? Why this waste of time on scruples?

To M. Leonor de San Gabriel at Córdoba
> Madrid, July. Year unknown.

Your letter moved me with compassion for your trouble. I grieve for you, for the harm it may cause not only your spiritual but your bodily health. Believe me, I do not think you have reason to feel this deep distress.

To Doña Juana de Pedraza, at Granada

Segovia, 28 January 1589

Cling to nothing, for if you pray faithfully God will look after your affairs – they have no master other than God nor can they have. . . . If [your letters] were not so minute, I'd like it better!

To Doña Juana de Pedraza, at Granada

Segovia, 12 October 1589

(Doña Juana fears the Saint has forgotten her.)

It would deeply distress me to think you believe what you say. It would be too bad after the many tokens of kindness you have shown me when I least deserved them. I am very far from having forgotten you. How could I forget someone as close to my heart as you are? While you walk in this darkness, in this desolation, this spiritual poverty you imagine that everyone and everything are failing you. And no wonder, for at such times you feel that God too is deserting you. But nothing is deserting you . . . Who are you to be worrying about yourself? A fine state you'll be in if you do that.

To María de la Encarnación at Segovia

Madrid, 6 July 1591

Where there is no love, put love and you will find love. . .

Excerpts from letters written by St Teresa of Ávila

To Don Alonso Álvarez Ramirez, Ávila

Valladolid, end of September 1568

Though he [St John of the Cross] is small in stature, he is great, I believe, in the sight of God.

To His Majesty King Philip II

Avila, 4 December 1577

This friar [St John of the Cross] is so weak from all his sufferings that I fear for his life. For the love of Our Lord, I implore your Majesty to command that he be released [from prison] immediately.

St John of the Cross as others remembered him

Fray John of the Cross would not allow it to be said that he was the founder of the Reform or even one of the two founders. If anyone mentioned such a thing he would reply, 'Nonsense.' Also, he was always glad to let others talk to persons of importance : content in the company of those of no account.

Fray Lucas de San José

He was exceptionally suited to hold a position of authority – he did so without loss of his extraordinary gentleness and courtesy.

ibid.

I heard him say one day in the presence of all the friars, that he blushed for shame when he recalled the mistakes he had made during his tenure of office. In fact, he had a flair for exercising authority.

ibid.

He exemplified goodness of every kind, especially charity towards his neighbour: he helped others in all their needs, spiritual and material, with solicitude and concern, in so far as their state and profession allowed. He paid particular attention to the needs of those under him, loving and helping them in every way that was appropriate.

Fray Diego de la Encarnación.

He was never idle. When he had time to spare he would spend it writing, or he would ask for the key of the convent garden, go out and uproot weeds. Sometimes, too, he was busy making walls and floors in our convent. If he had a companion he took him with him; if not, he asked some of the sisters to help.

M. Magdalena del Espíritu Santo.

When leaving Beas to return to his monastery at Monte Calvario he said to the nuns, 'If I don't come back, imitate the sheep – ruminate on what I have said while I was with you.'

P. Alonso de la Madre de Dios.

He lived in hope and hope sustained him.

Fray Juan Evangelista.

At recreation, though he talked about God, he made us laugh. Also we loved to go out with him.

ibid.

One day he went to the house of a person of importance to cast out a devil. Afterwards, when he had gone, the devil said: 'O dear me, I can't get the better of this little friar nor find a way to bring about his downfall. For years he has been persecuting me at Ávila, Torafe and here!'

I told the Father about this. Whereupon he said, 'O rubbish! You can't believe the devil. All he says is lies.'

ibid.

Sayings attributed to St John of the Cross

If you fear not to fall alone, how can you presume to rise alone? Think how much more can be achieved by two together than by one by himself!

S.S.M.

Mine are the heavens and mine the earth. Mine are the people: the righteous are mine and sinners are mine. God himself is mine and for me, for Christ is mine and all for me. What then, my soul, do you ask for? What do you seek? All this is yours, all for you.

ibid.

Strive to be at peace in your heart. Let nothing that comes to pass in this world disturb you – remember that all things come to an end.

ibid.

Let all find compassion in you.

ibid.

He who is alone with none at hand to support and guide him is like a tree that stands isolated in a field, owned by no one. However much fruit it bears, passers-by will strip it and it will not mature.

ibid.

Though the road be straightforward and easy for those of good will, he who travels alone will not get far and will endure much discomfort unless he has good feet, courage and the perseverance that goes with courage.

ibid.

As the fly that clings to honey hinders itself from escaping, so the soul that clings to spiritual sweetness hinders freedom and contemplation.

ibid.

The devil resorts to many wiles to lead astray those who would live a spiritual life. He deceives them under the guise not of what appears evil but what appears good.

ibid.

Do not take a man as an example to follow, however holy he be, for the devil will set his faults before you. Imitate only Christ, who is the sum of perfection and holiness. Then you cannot go astray.

P.L.

He who loves not his neighbour hates God.

S.S.M.

It is better to curb the tongue than to fast on bread and water.

ibid.

The soul that walks in love neither causes weariness nor does it become weary.

P.L.

Love consists not in great feelings, but in detachment and in suffering for the beloved.

ibid.

At eventide, you will be judged on love.

S.S.M.

SELECT BIBLIOGRAPHY

Writings of St John of the Cross

Obras de San Juan de la Cruz, edition and notes by P. Silverio de Santa Teresa, C.D., Burgos.

Works of St John of the Cross, translated and edited by E. Allison Peers from the critical editions of P. Silverio de Santa Teresa, C.D.; three vols in one, Anthony Clarke Books, Wheathampstead, Herts.

Relevant Books

P. Bruno de Jesús Maria, C.D., *Saint Jean de la Croix*, Preface by Jacques Maritain, Paris 1929; English translation London 1932.

P. Crisógono de Jesús, C.D., *Vida de San Juan de la Cruz*, Madrid 1955; English translation London 1958.

P. Efrén de la Madre de Dios, C.D., *Tiempo y Vida de Santa Teresa*, Madrid 1968.

E. Allison Peers, *Handbook to the Life and Times of St Teresa and St John of the Cross*, London 1954.

E. Allison Peers, *St John of the Cross and Other Lectures and Addresses*, London 1946.

E. Allison Peers, *Spirit of the Flame*, London 1943.

A Benedictine of Stanbrook, *Medieval Mystical Tradition and St John of the Cross*, London 1953.

Frs Thomas and Gabriel, O.D.C. (editors), *Teresa of Ávila, Studies in Her Life*, Dublin 1963.

Gerald Brenan, *St John of the Cross, His Life and Poetry*, Cambridge 1973, paperback edition 1975.